LENAR SHAYEH

# ONE SONG
# WILL BE ENOUGH

*Stories, interviews*

*London 2023*

Published by Hertfordshire Press Ltd © 2023
e-mail: publisher@hertfordshirepress.com
www.hertfordshirepress.com

LENAR SHAYEH

# ONE SONG
# WILL BE ENOUGH

*Stories, interviews*

English

Editor Gareth Stamp
Translators Alexey Sakharov, Tatyana Kazachenko
Typeset Daniel Brown

*British Library Catalogue in Publication Data
A catalogue record for this book is available from the British Library
Library of Congress in Publication Data
A catalogue record for this book has been requested*

ISBN: 978-1-913356-65-1

*Vladimir Schastny Award for the category "Heritage"*
*of the Open Eurasian Literary Festival & Book Forum - 2022*

## ABOUT VLADIMIR SCHASTNY

Vladimir Schastny (pseudonyms: Vladimir Drozdov, Uladzimir Skolski) - Belarusian statesman, diplomat, writer, critic, translator was born on November 25, 1948 in the city of Smorgon. In his school years, he showed interest and abilities in foreign languages, which determined his future path. In 1972, he graduated from the Minsk Pedagogical Institute of Foreign Languages and successfully completed an internship in Pakistan. In 1976-1977 he worked as a teacher in his native pedagogical institute, with pleasure sharing knowledge with students. In 1978, Vladimir graduated from the UN courses at the Moscow Institute of Foreign Languages named after M. Torez and entered the Russian translation service of the UN Secretariat in New York, where he worked until 1982. He also worked in various positions in the Ministry of Foreign Affairs of the Republic of Belarus.

However, Mr. Schastny's contemporaries remembered him not only as a statesman. Many colleagues recall his trembling attitude towards art. In artistic translation, he worked since 1977 - translated from English and Urdu into Belarusian. He was the author of articles on cultural issues, the history of fine arts. Translated by Vladimir Schastny, the book of prose by K. McAlers "The Ballad of the Sad Cafe" (1988), the collection "American Detective Narrative" (1993), some works by E. Poe, E. S. Gardner and others were published. Mr. Schastny is also the author of dramatic works staged by the National Academic Theater named after J. Kolos, books "Artists of the Paris School from Belarus: essays, biographies, a guide" (2012), "Paris," "Albatrosses," the catalog of the exhibition "Artists of the Paris School from Belarus" (21.9.2012—14.1.2013 in Minsk). In addition, Vladimir became one of the ideological inspirers of the 'Art-Belarus' project. His efforts to popularize and return the names of world famous native artists of Belarus formed the basis of the project and made a significant contribution to the return of masterpieces of artists of the Paris School to the country. He laid the ideological foundation for the formation of the Belgazprombank corporate collection, which today is recognized as one of the largest collections of the works of expressionists of the Paris School not only in Belarus, but also in Eastern and Central Europe as a whole. Many of the works of art in the collection were included in 2012 in the Republican List of Historical and Cultural Heritage of Belarus.

In addition, Vladimir was enthusiastically engaged in the reconstruction of the Oginsky estate in Zalessk. As chairman of the national commission of UNESCO, he did everything possible to restore the estate and revive it. In 2003, he initiated the international conference "Historical Estates. State and prospects, "as well as the preparation, with the assistance of UNESCO, of documents for the restoration of the former estate of Mr. Oginsky and the receipt of a copy of the composer's archive from the State Archive of Ancient Acts in Moscow. He obtained the publication of 4 volumes of Memoirs of Michal Oginsky translated from French, "History of Poland and the Poles from 1788 to 1815." He bequeathed to the museum-estate of Mr. Oginsky his own rich collection of historical maps of the XVII-XX centuries, which he collected for many years.

This is not a complete list of those undertakings of Vladimir Schastny, who made an invaluable contribution to the development of the historical heritage of culture and art of Belarus. For his work, he was awarded the Francis Skorina Medal in 2009 and the Certificate of Honor of the Council of Ministers of the Republic of Belarus in 1998 and 2006.

# CONTENT

# STORIES

# MY HEART IS BURNING WITH FIRE

## *Prologue*

At first glance, the construction of hydroelectric power stations in the USSR beginning in the 60s and 70s (of the last century) made it possible to provide the population with all necessary electrical activity. On the other hand, huge areas of fertile land, hayfields and meadows, were flooded to facilitate their construction: many villages and settlements sinking underwater. Sometimes, because of inaccuracies in the calculations – and following the forced relocation of villages to empty, ruined landscapes – the imprisoned water did not even complete its assigned task. If one thinks about it, only in the territory of the Aktanysh district of the Republic of Tatarstan, did large villages, such as Old and New Semiostrov (Osher and Chiyalek) and the Tatar Asbey, Derbeshki settlement (in which were thousands of houses), fall victim to this issue due to the fact they disappeared from the face of the earth. Oh, how many tears, regrets, how many curses, causing, perhaps, the forced and violent breakup of native homes were witnessed? Anyway, I want to tell you about the Old Semiostrov. This is the native village of my Deu-eni[1] and many of my relatives. After all, it is so close and dear to me.

Of course, I had heard that Gabdulla-abziy[2] was still living there, but I did not see him with my own eyes. As they say, native blood calls. Nevertheless, I visited the village from where my lineage originates.

# 1

I remember this day very clearly. Yet, it was August 30th when I initially set off from the village of Taktalachik. It was morning. First, I stopped at the village of Kart, then, in the evening, I traveled through the village of Bulyek, before heading for the village of Yamaly. Following this, the Old Semiostrov. Once there, oddly, the sun seemed unusually hot. Indeed, there were no clouds in the sky. With hindsight, it was only after getting out of Yamaly to the boundless savannah that a cool breeze started to blow. All evening, I walked and walked; looking at the far horizon, until something white appeared in the distance. Possibly, this is a lonely house? Either way, I managed to take a photo, while continuing to move ahead. Surprisingly, there was not a single soul on the steppe. Occasionally, a car would pass, lifting dust into the air of a dirty road. But, by Allah, the white colour turned out to be a pile of fertilizer towering in the distance! So, where is the village? Where is the earth that attracts my soul? The land of my grandparents? Anyway, I am walking and walking, although along an endless road. Then, a forest appeared ahead, even though it seemed far away. I noticed weeping willows bending into the

---

1       *Deu-eni (in Tatar)* – maternal grandmother.
2       *Abziy (in Tatar)* – a respectful appeal to a man, older in age.

water, wherein something black flashed... Wasn't it Gylmetdin-babay[3] come out to meet his grandson? His missing heart still sought? But, I was told he went blind after his return from prison: a man, slandered by fists. Suddenly thereafter, I remembered a story told by the daughter of Gayfetdin-aby[4] a relative of my Deu-eni, Flyuda-apa[5].

"...*They said that from us (from the dead village of Kart) to the Old Semiostrov was eight miles. But, Gylmetdin-babay was blind. I do not even remember him ever having good vision. When I visited, he used to cry, stroking my face and moving his hand over me. As for, Gainiyamal-ebi[6] she was very affectionate and loved to sing. I still remember how she sang:*
*"I went to my home for a long time,*
*Because I got tired on my way.*
*However, someone sits – plunged into thoughts,*
*Because my heart is burning with fire".*
*Very sweet, but the dead woman smiled..."*

Oh Allah, are they waiting for me there; looking through their window? Either way, Gainiyamal-ebi cooked a delicious balesh[7], boiled in a samovar on coals: all made fragrant, with Oregano, Lime flowers and Dog Rose tea. Why, however, don't I know Gylmetdin-babay, or Gainiyamal-ebi better? Why didn't they wait for my birth? Who is to blame for the fact I am forever deprived of the opportunity to see the village of Old Semiostrov? Why did you two deprive me, why?

As I walked along with such thoughts (wiping my tears away), that black object became clearly visible. It was a rusted iron pillar. Moreover, on approaching it, some individual letters became visible, then words appeared. Finally, I almost reached it: only two, or three, steps being

---

3       *Babay (in Tatar)* – grandfather.
4       *Aby (in Tatar)* – uncle.
5       *Apa (in Tatar)* – aunt.
6       *Ebi (in Tatar)* – grandmother.
7       *Balesh (in Tatar)* – a large round pie with potatoes and meat; Tatar national dish..

left. On one side of the pillar was written «The Old Semiostrov», while on the other, «The New Semiostrov». Oddly, these words pierced my soul as though everything was upset inside me. I felt so good, but at the same time sad. However, there was little choice other than to follow the direction indicated by the arrow on the column. So, I turned left. Thence, after strolling a little, I reached a lake. It was surrounded on each side by Willows standing like grandmothers gathered for party, as well as Reeds and Water-lilies (on the surface of the water), peeking out to see me, whilst seeming to say: " Welcome, brother! Go down the road. Do not abandon it, or you will get lost" . Curiously, on the other side of the lake, a herd of cows was grazing as three shepherds spu n fabric near a haystack. I tried asking them: " Hey, am I going in the right direction to get to the Old Semiostrov?" But, my question was only heard by a powerful wind. So, instead of sounds, my words and letters flew and dived into the water, or hu ng on the willows, or reached up to strike the cow's horns. Ah, did anyone hear any words when the elderly lamented during their forced resettlement of the village? Loudly, they cried: " We didn't want to move. This is our native land, our home: we were born here and will die here" at the same time as perplexed: youngsters rejoined: " We hoped to live here, to have families, raise children" – albeit, to deaf ears and blinded eyes.

Suddenly, a tractor appeared from somewhere. Allah is Gracious! A man and a woman sat in the cab. A small cart was attached behind the tractor. I raised my hand and asked the driver:

– Abzyi, is it far to the Old Semiostrov? How can I get to Gabdulla-aby's house?

– " Haydi, get on the cart", he waved his hand, pointing backwards. I jumped up immediately.

After some time of shaking on the tractor's cart, the iron horse finally stopped at a haystack. So, descending from the cab, the abziy showed me the way:

– " There, do you see an iron pillar? From thence begins the village of Old Semiostrov. Do you see a house a little further? This is the house of Gabdulla. Go straight along the road ahead" .

Without a second chance to say thank you, each of them threw down forks from the cart and hurriedly began to load the hay.

Curiously, I recall that when the cemetery of Old Semiostrov was moved, they dug up the graves of our ancestors as quickly; filled up boxes with bones and carried them out on the same tractors. Some wondered if the bones wouldn't turn into ash after such shaking, but they didn't disintegrate.

Anyway, in the distance, a tin roof glinted. It marked the presence of a lonely house greeting me. At the same time, a strong wind seemed like the song of Gainiyamal-eby singing in my ear:

*" I went to my home for a long time,*
*Because I got tired on my way… "*

…Yet, we cannot waste time, even though our legs are exhausted. We must go forward, forever forward, to the Old Semiostrov.

**2**

…That observed, opposite me was an iron pillar on which large letters read: " The Old Semiostrov". Behind it thickets of Nettles, Burdock, Flax and Wormwood were rustling, while through this " forest " (which is my height) a narrow path could be seen.

It turned out this is the village. Yet, I did not want to see it like this. If only I could enter the courtyard of the house of Gylmetdin-babay and Gayniyamal-ebi to drink a sip of cold water from a deep well… Something now i mpossible. Actually, even the locations of their houses could only be guessed at nowadays. Relatedly, observers know that up to one's death, one desires to drink before the tongue clings to the palate.

Hence, with a modicum of dread, I stepped onto the path. I moved deeper and deeper into the environment. It appeared strange that no one could say there was once a big village of seven hundred yards; with a dairy factory, a shop, a mill and other farm buildings. Currently, only an overgrown wasteland with weeds and grass remains. All meaning, this " forest" of Nettles, Burdock and Wormwood perpetually rumbles, as if someone was walking through it. Perhaps the past was watching me? Anyway, I noticed high stems of dry grass waving in the wind, rustling, as if they were singing. Almost, telling me the history of village life. They whispered something they wanted to tell me. Also, winding paths along a forgotten street to vegetable gardens lead me to the central part of our former village. Here, probably, stood the farm of Gabdeljebbar-agay[8], whilst over there Malik-babay, had a daughter. Additionally, I recall a rich man named Munavar living nearby? Oh sweet village, you are like a lonely old woman waiting for her last hours. I hear your heavy breathing. But, how can you survive when your history, the whole of your previous life, was crushed with rocks and weedy grass? Contrarily, I know you do not want to die, to disappear like the morning mist, melting into an autumnal breeze. Please don't break away from your roots. Just try to live!

All in all, I walked for a long time. Then, suddenly, an open area appeared before my eyes on the right of the lake. There was also a meadow towards the right, while to the left there was a sagging shed. Further on, the heart of the village could be calculated by a skeletal farmhouse without any fence. An unexpected solid against otherwise ghostly structures. In any case, this newly built timbered house had absorbed the whole history of the village: particularly, perhaps, in features like the bathhouse, wood-burning stove, its thatched roof, the heaps of logs, fenced enclosure and

---

8     *Agay (in Tatar)* – a respectful appeal to a man, older in age.

carefully defined garden. Clearly, poultry were milling around, cows chewed as they rested in the cover, horses snorted with happy exhaustion from the heat, whilst bleating sheep etched a seemingly traditional landscape.

Disconcertingly, when I went into the yard, a middle-aged woman appeared from nowhere. She has a colourful dress with short sleeves and dark blue pants, a neatly tied (but motley) kerchief on her head, which crowned a face that was surprised to see me.

– " Hello! Is Gabdulla-aby here?" I asked.

– " Yes, he is here. I'm his little sister from the city of Sarapul. My name is Gluda. Every summer I come back to my native village. Who are you?"

– " Lenar. My Deu-eni Gulchira is the daughter of Gylmetdin from this village. I've wanted to see you for a long time' , I answered. " But where is Gabdulla-aby?"

– " Stacking hay in the back of the garden, I'll call now" , said Gluda-apa and disappeared. Afterwards, a grandmother came out of the old house wearing glasses, a worn blue blouse, as well as a long dress faded from continual washing. Weirdly, her head was covered with a simple kerchief, which deliberately contrasted with the rest of her appearance. Obviously, it was Gabdulla's mother, Guljan-ebi. In a sense, she seemed the same age as the crooked, retired, house behind her. A state of affairs asking how there could be a future without a past; a present without any history?

In addition, two men soon appeared from the garden; their faces and hands badly sunburnt. One was wearing a T-shirt under his uniform, along with a hat on his head. The second sported a long-sleeved shirt and a grey cap. Unarguably, more relaxed in his dress, the latter turned out to be Gabdulla-aby himself. Thus, I greeted them and explained why I had come.

– " Very good, very good" , smiled my host.

Then, with their friend Revis-abziy, they elegantly started to smoke. In that instant, Gluda-apa quickly ran to the old house to make tea, while Guljan-ebi went to the lakeside to look after the sheep. However, we, the lucky men, stayed together.

– " Glory to Allah, in spite of the fact this village has disappeared; the people continue" , Gabdulla-aby began.

– " Relatives and friends visit the village. They come from Chally, Bugulme and Sarapul[9] by cars. They come for fishing. Every year with our fellow countrymen we spend Sabantuy[10] together" , he continued. " Indeed, since 1976, we have been abandoned, but yet we live. Are you unable to leave your native land?" he sighed heavily. It was as if these scenarios repeated endlessly. The same characters, events, and even words, caught in the ceaseless eddies of time itself.

– " Do you have as much love for your native village, Gabdulla-aby?"

– " What if water hadn't flooded?" I asked.

– " Ah, brother, the wishes of our Father and Mother are able to protect us from water and fire. Also, I too did not want to part from my native land. That special place wherein my childhood and youth had passed. I still did not want to... Even though water once flooded thereabouts. Anyway, why was it necessary to destroy the whole village? There was a time when it occupied eighty, to ninety, hectares of land. Now, they just count the dead. Thus , our words are full of sadness, whilst a poor man's heart is forever weak; he cries with bitter tears" . Tellingly, I could say nothing.

– " The transfer was paid, of course, but even money could not replace our log cabins. They had already been disassembled. I, from the very beginning, grabbed our grounds with tooth and nail, yet could not imagine anything other than my drowned aul". He sighed with sorrow,

---

9        *Chally, Bugulme (in Tatar)* – cities of the Republic of Tatarstan. *Sarapul* is a city in the Republic of Udmurtia.

10        *Sabantuy (in Tatar)* – ancient Tatar national holiday.

and finished his cigarette. " In the summer the authorities helped Revis, who is the son of our sister Dilaris. It's good they are alive . Praise Allah, mother is still alive" .

– " And not alone?" I whimsically replied. " Do you want to leave everything behind you?"

– " I'm used to it already. My legs do not want me to walk to a foreign land, despite the number of advisers surrounding us. Move, do not be stupid" they say. " But, even now, if they start punishing me, I will not agree. Until my last breath, I'll stay here" .

– " This is your house, it's an antique. Probably, from the regal times?"

– " Yes, the house was built in 1918, although it was not the main house. We lived in it for half a century. That's why it is so valuable. We had bought it in 1959. From then onwards, we developed it. In summer we live in the old apartments; we move to the modern rooms in winter".

Then , Glyuda-apa called us to drink tea. So, after washing our hands we all went into the low house.

In the front corner on the table there was a samovar on coals. At first, I thought they did not have any light, or any gas. In which case, they were deprived of all modern facilities. Yet, no one would dream of exchanging their native land for contemporary conveniences. After all, if lost even once, it will never return. Either way, we were happy to talk and drink tea.

– " I assume you have not drunk this kind of tea before?" grinned Revis-aby.

– " Actually, I have, albeit, ten, or fifteen years ago. However, since that time, I have been treated by our neighbor (now deceased) Makhinur-ebi to similar, if not the same, brews. But, I haven't before had the opportunity to drink tea boiled in a samovar on charcoal". Following this exchange, I drank with pleasure; wiping away the drops of sweat that appeared on my forehead. Curiously, the tea was so fragrant and tasty it seemed the wells, or streams, sourcing this water had been touched by an angel's wing.

– " Our water is from lake Sadak. I do not have time to dig for new wells ", Gabdulla-aby added, whilst also wiping sweat from his brow.

Thereafter, Guljan-ebi came in. Exhausted by the heat, she sat down on a bed near to her.

Eventually though, I needed to say goodbye and went out of the house. Strangely, after drinking this powerful tea, everything appeared purer and lighter in my soul – as if a warm summer rain had fallen from the sky. Synchronously, the fascinating trills of larks were heard as I sensed these expansions. Oh, how could one leave such a beautiful village? Unarguably, it is the source of dreams calling to its scattered citizens: a reservoir of weeping weeds testifying to the cyclic reappearance of this phantasmagorical land. I scrambled, therefore, to the top fence of the paddock and looked around in order to get a feeling of orientation. Oh, what beauty! Divine! I saw Hayfields, horses, and cisterns ! All amazingly preserved! As the Tatar people's poet Gamil Afzal wrote,

> " Tighten up the song in full voice.
> How well this would be!
> Having risen even higher to sing:
> The world is beautiful! The world is wide!"

Truly, one must only look at this village from above to know it like the palm of one's hand. Perhaps this elation is why I returned to say my goodbyes.

Arriving back, I noticed Guljan-ebi and Glyuda-apa stepping into the courtyard, while wiping their wet faces with handkerchiefs. So, we sat together on a bench opposite the new house as others came and went in the manner of shadows. Nevertheless, our conversation started.

— " In 1930 I came here as a bride. From that time onward, I have not wetted my best shoes: either accidentally, or in times of flood" , Guljan-ebi said with pride and resentment.

— " Do you live here in winter, too?" I asked:

— " Yes, although for necessary purchases, I sleigh once a week to our neighbouring village of Yamaly. In the summer slightly less often. Why are you surprised?" Gabdulla-aby looked at me questioningly.

— " Once there was a brick factory, and a factory for processing sunflower oil. Also, rabbit and poultry farms worked in full force. If one thinks about it, one is amazed" , said Glyuda-apa. Yet, the words of Guljan-ebi simply raised new questions:

— " Elders said that in 1914 the village was flooded. Back then, people moved by boat. They visited each other on the wooden platforms. Nonetheless, there were no hydroelectric power stations in those days…"

Overall, we sat and talked, until a T-40 tractor rumbled along in the far distance – a sign Dilaris was arriving. Inexplicably, this sound equally alerted me to the fact the sun was descending towards sunset, whilst the birdhouses were filling with residents. Hence, I asked Gabdulla-aby:

— " Do starlings, like people, keep returning here?" At which, I thought I heard a voice reply, " With the arrival of spring, they return every year. Each dawn they begin to sing their beautiful, melodic songs"

…Finally, having said goodbye to everyone, I started on my way home. However, standing at Sadak lake (which was located nearby), I became thoughtful before continuing along the road. Certainly, I knew the heart of the village was still beating, albeit with difficulty. Additionally, I understood breathing means life in a place where starlings perpetually return. Yet, possibly, the village had become a recurrent dreamscape: a ghostly Brigadoon existing only in the imagination? Or was it merely a tragic casualty of abortive planning? Ah, farewell my dear heart. This holy land of Old Semiostrov! But not forever! This may be my first visit, although it will not be my last. You and I will see each other again!

# Epilogue

This is the end of my journey, even though, that evening when the herd returned, I visited Chiber-apa[11] – who lives in Yamaly. A trek adding another 15 km to my expedition, although not a single extra gasp on top of my exhaustion. At eleven o'clock I finally arrived back in Taktalachik – to witness new houses being built. However, we need the past. All explaining why there are people wishing to reside in Old Semiostrov – and always will be. A truth taking the pain out of Gainiyamal-ebi's sad song when it sounds in my ears during anxious nights...

> " *I went to my home for a long time,*
> *Because I got tired on my way.*
> *However, someone sits – plunged into thoughts,*
> *Because my heart is burning with fire*".

---

11     *Chiber-apa (in Tatar)* – literally: Beautiful aunt.

# TWO STORIES

Strange thoughts pop into my head. I recall different stories, which contradict each other drastically. But it's life, and anything can happen in it – dark or light, bitter or sweet… You never know.

## 1

Autumn. The end of October. A fairy-tale mysterious day. Covering the streets of Kazan, which previously suffered from long rains that washed away the autumn unattractiveness seven times, the white stars of snow fall quietly from the skies. Such a wonderful day! Charming… Even looking at it is pure delight!

The two – a lad and a girl – are walking along the alley of a park. The road before them is radiating with paths – to the right and to the left, the straight and the curvy ones. The lad is cheerful and the girl is sad, his face is happy and hers is not.

" Let's stop here," suggested Galiya suddenly.

They stopped at the crossing of three roads.

" What happened? " asked Halil perplexedly.

" I think of our future, " began the girl in a somewhat cold and dull voice. " It bothers me."

" I love you. What else matters? We will surely be happy. Inshallah, we will get married as soon as this summer. We are finishing the fourth course, after all…"

" I will not marry you," she stated resolutely.

" What do you mean?!"

Think of it, Halil. What have you got? No car, no flat. Not even a one-room one. Your parents are paupers. As they say, neither house nor home. I think love is not the most important thing. My parents raised me not to suffer my entire life, having fallen in love with a Dzhigit, doing their best to ensure my well-being. We cannot be together…"

Something strange has happened to Halil. Suddenly it seemed that soot began falling from the blue hazy skies. It made Galiya dirty from head to foot. It smutted her face and her clothes… Even the bluish-green eyes of the girl became black.

…At the left, across the road, standing by the gorgeous car was Ismaghil, a handsome guy in stylish clothes.

" Where are you, Galiya?" he shouted through the snow fog. " Are you coming with me or not?"

" Coming," responded the girl and, having looked at the pale Halil, said: " I'm not an Englishwoman. I don't have a habit of disappearing without saying goodbye. Farewell, Halil. I go. Your Galiya will live a comfortable life."

The girl ran to the left - towards Ismaghil, who was smiling j ibingly.

They went out of the park and got into a posh car. The car vanished leaving behind it a gold silvery whirlwind.

Halil remained standing on the crossing of three roads. It is commonly believed that Dzhigits do not cry. And he did not, but he plunged into his grief like he was insane. He felt bad. Halil did not know what to do with himself. He looked around with a glassy, faded stare. At that moment it seemed to him that his life was over and that nothing good could happen to him in the future… Halil cast a cold glance at the curvy road that was turning to the right. The lad knew that it ended with a deep ravine, almost an abyss. Without hesitation he rushed there like a mad racer. Here it is, salvation , so close. Fifteen steps... ten... Now it will all be resolved, and the earth will welcome him into its embrace.

Five steps... Blast it all! Three steps… Two... One… Half a step...

Suddenly he heard a nice girlish voice.

" Stop! What are you doing?!"

The voice was so kind, so tender…

Who is that? But it was already impossible for him to stop. It was too late. Halil was falling down... But suddenly his heart revolted, and he felt a strong urge to live. Halil caught hold of a pipe that poked out from the steep slope and looked under his feet. The depth of the ravine was endless. Its bottom was filled with scrap iron and huge boulders... "Ah, I want to live so much!"

The lad pulled himself up holding the pipe as if it was a crossbar and managed to get to the snow-white vista . There was no girl around. But her tender voice was still ringing in his ears. Who was she? A harpi from paradise?.. A guardian angel?.. Why did she address him?.. Why did she stop him?.. Or, maybe, it was only his imagination?.. But no matter who she was, the main thing was that he was alive!.. Alive!.. Halil shook himself free from the ground and began to walk along the straight road, having soon disappeared in the snow fog…

2

The old Karima-ebi was watching the snowflakes falling quietly through the small half-frozen window of her rickety log-house. Today she was saying good-bye to her eightieth autumn. The old woman took a copybook from a dusty chest, in which she was making notes from as early as she was young. The diary changed but very little, it did not even turn yellow over all these years. She was turning its leaves, feeling sad, and again and again was raising her eyes at the window.

Indeed, there was a time when the aul was full of life. So many young people there were in it! The old Gapsalyam, who has been dead for ten years already, was growing up in this very house. Karima was eighteen when he brought her here from the next house. They lived in perfect harmony with Gapsalyam. She always busied herself so cheerfully about the house! Eight children were born one after another. It was so good. Little children were growing up, spreading their wings, then started to fly away to the city, which was crowded with people like a beehive. Even the last, the youngest son decided not to stay. He left his father and mother, his native home, in which he was born and where he grew up; he left the beautiful river, Agidel, with its curvy course, the Kashlak Forest, the golden fields of rye… How could they exchange this divine beauty for something else!? What about the broad fields, the tugays? The pastures?.. It is impossible to understand children. What was that that they missed? Why don't they come to visit their lonely old mother? Why don't they show any interest in how she lives? Karima-ebi felt very, very lonely. She has neither neighbours, nor relatives in the village. The only thing she has is a cemetery, where her Gapsalyam, her mother, father, her grandfather and grandmother lie. But no one comes back from there.

…For over eight decades the sweet-smelling smoke was trailing continuously from the chimney of a house that went down into the soil like an old curved pine tree. Now it's all over. No one will ever learn how sweet was the smell of the oak logs that were once burning in the village stove...

Two stories. Both are about ordinary people, about our fates. Life is not as easy as a pie. It would be good if everybody could live their lives happily and without remorse...

# BAL-BABAY

My dear daughter child, come, take my prayer. For the good memory of myself.' Having said that, Bal-Babay[12] put into the hands of his grand-daughter a sheet of paper with an Arabic text that was neatly folded into four. The paper was yellowish and its edges were a bit ragged. Believe in Allah, my dear child. He does exist, Allah... Be a firm Muslim. Muslim religion is the only quality that preserves Tatarness... Here, take it. My grandfather wrote it to me when I was a boy. I've been keeping it for ninety years in memory of him…"

" Why do you say so, granddad? We will meet again, won't we? " said the surprised Sylu, who came to visit him.

Who knows…"

No, no, granddad!.. Don't you even think of it. Alright?.." said the girl and embraced Bal-Babay tight. Tears welled in the eyes of Sylu, and anxiety creeped in to her soul...

...Bal-Babay was old. In these recent times he himself began thinking of it more and more often. It had been ten years after his wife died. He had no close relatives. They say that the one who is the only survivor lives the lives of those who have passed away. Can it be true? Soon he will turn ninety five years old... These years were not full of joy but grief, of worries and troubles...

---

12      *Bal (in Tatar)* – honey; *Babay (in Tatar)* – granddad.

Deportation of the family from the native village during the collectivisation, the loss of his father, who was taken away by men in ' black hats' and got lost forever; the Great Patriotic War, falling prisoner. Coming back home elated, back to the motherland , and, what a pity: sentencing to ten years of imprisonment... – all this has left deep wounds in the heart of Bal-Babay. To top it all, his elder daughter, Nourlybika, married a Russian. She did not even listen to her father, but just went away with an infidel. Bal-Babay felt bad for her for a long time. His heart was aching. He was exhausted. With time he seemed to have accepted it, but in his heart he did not, and did not regard her with favour...

There he is again, flashing among the beehives opposite his house. He is dressed in a show-white gown and a veil of the same colour. In his hands he holds, as always, a fumigator. The sweet smell of smoke from touchwood fills the entire garden.

Bal-Babay is the nickname he was given in the post-war years. Slandered as a public enemy, unjustly convicted, when he came home following ten years of ordeals, he could not find a job – no one hired him. That is why, having eventually found some separate cloud of bees, he became a bee-keeper. That was how he found a job for himself...

But today Bal-Babay was in high spirits. As if in the years of his youth, he is running from one beehive to another. He opens a beehive and, talking to bees, checks the honeycombs, then he sprays it with the sweet-smelling smoke and closes the lid quickly. When doing so, he is constantly singing in a soft voice, as if ready to break into a dance any minute...

> *Sweet and full-flavoured honey,*
> *But don't eat too much of it.*
> *The restless bee only loves those*
> *Who are of its kind...*

Watching Bal-Babay busying himself by an old apple-tree, was the surprised Gulsum, who popped in to visit her father. She could hardly imagine her father was such a cheerful and merry man!.. What a surprise!..

*The little bee collects the honey,*
*" It's sweet" – she does not boast of it.*
*She flaps away the wasps and flies,*
*And makes no friends with gadflies…*

Singing so, Bal-Babay was leaving the garden when he met his daughter. " What if father went slightly crazy" , she thought to herself. Father, what are you doing? Oh, my God, has anything happened?.."

No, my dear child, my little star, nothing has happened. Just felt like singing."

He loved Gulsum. Maybe because she was his last-born child, or maybe because she resembled him most of all, but Bal-Babay liked her most. Nourlybika went to Siberia and got lost there. Does not even come to visit him... Indeed, will she come to her father with her Tanya and Zhenya who don't know a word in their mother tongue?!

...Gulsum left him when it got dark. Bal-Babay looked into her eyes and embraced her tight with the words " my dear child" . They stood like this for quite a long time, unable to tear away from one another...

Alright, father. So, you say you will not go to the wedding of Ilghiz?.. He is kind of your favourite grandson... Perhaps, you could come…"

I said once and don't feel like repeating. N-O spells no…"

Well, you know better, father. Take care. I will come again tomorrow to visit you…"

Farewell, my dear child, my little star…"

As Gulsum went out of the gate, Bal-Babay followed her with his eyes. After that he stood still for a while; then sighed heavily. Having entered the house, he roamed from one room to another for a long time.

Although it was midnight he once again looked at the beehives. It was amazingly quiet all over the world. Not even a leaf would rustle. Not even a sound would be heard...

They sleep... All are sleeping tight..." he said to himself. He wanted to smile with all his heart, but his eyes somehow did not smile...

* * *

Early in the morning Gulsum hurried to visit her father again. She felt at heart some cold, some shapeless emptiness. " Maybe father would change his mind. Maybe he would come to the wedding of Ilghiz and Olga. Would bless them , - she thought.

The door was open. There was some cold silence in the house. Some strange silence... Gulsum ran about the rooms like crazy, but did not find father. On the table in the upper room she found an old sheet of paper with yellowish edges, which was neatly folded into four. Just a few words on it: " Sorry. Can't stand it..."

...The same very moment the heart of Gulsum sunk. Tears welled in her eyes, and her lips trembled. She could not utter a word, because on the old apple-tree opposite the window there hung something that resembled a human body. And it was only that bees were flying around it, buzzing, as if wanting to tell something to him...

# HANDKERCHIEF

Gamil was vexed. He flew into the house, having banged the door behind him. He passed by the house of Nafisa several times, but failed to see the girl. But he needed to see her even with the corner of his eye. He needed it badly. Yesterday they met by the spring, but they did not manage to talk. The conversation was flagging. They just stood looking at each other, not knowing what to say, until the girl finally said in a shy voice: " I need to go. Mother has probably already lost me" .

" Could you stay just a bit more?" – said Gamil. " Ok, then" , – answered the girl timidly.

Despite the yesterday's meeting, he was already missing her. What is happening to him? Can it be love? The only thing he could think of was of her, of his Nafisa. Her black eyes, like small pieces of coal, her long, blue-black hair, which made her look like a Bashkir, her mysterious laughter, her look that makes his head swimming. It seemed that love has weaved its nest in the heart of the lad, in which there were only two of them – him and her.

Gamil wanted to marvel at a handkerchief with a flower of tulip that was embroidered on it. It was a gift from Nafisa. He opened the door of a cabinet... But, where is the handkerchief? Gamil has just recently washed and ironed it so that not a wrinkle could be found on it, and put it into the chest pocket of a white shirt. The lad has turned the entire cabinet upside down. The handkerchief has disappeared. He searched the chest and the nightstand… How can it be?! He put the valueless gift of Nafisa into his pocket with his own hands! The handkerchief is so dear to him!

Gamil was running about the house. No handkerchief on the book shelf either. He rushed to his elder sister, Galiya:

Have you taken my handkerchief? Where did you put it to?.. Give it back!.. " he shouted.

As a crazy cock he was attacking his innocent sister paying no attention to her words:

Why should I know where your handkerchief is? "

It ended in him grasping the sewing machine of his sister who was not guilty of anything at all and banging it down on the floor. But the handkerchief still was not found.

Gamil felt like they had stolen his heart. His heart was filled with grief. Where to go? Where to search for it? He was unable to think straight…

Finally the lad could not stand it anymore. He got to the hayloft and spent a long time there, lying motionless, just sobbing. " How can it be?! I put it to the pocket of a shirt with my own hands" , – he murmured. Such a dear gift, the first handkerchief he received from his love…

…A year and a half later Gamil and Nafisa got married. They were happy. Then their first daughter was born.

One day Nafisa went to their neighbour, Khayat-apa. Her daughter left the village the next day after the wedding of Nafisa and Gamil. They said that she lived and worked in the city or somewhere else. Khayat-apa took from them a wooden cask for mead a year ago and has still not returned it. So Nafisa went for it herself.

Under the plug in the cask the young woman saw some yellowish piece of cloth. She picked it up… and encountered a flower of tulip embroidered on it! This is how her gift was found, which Gamil had lost so mysteriously.

# RASPBERRY

In high summer, in July of that year, it suddenly turned cold. Everything has changed just in an instant. Nature has drawn the autumn blanket early. The dull thunderclouds have hidden the hot rays of the sun. The bitter wind was blowing every day, and cold rain was falling down uninterruptedly every night. The garden hedge and the window frames have bulged because of the excess of moisture. Raspberries in the backyard, always before so large and juicy, have shrunken with cold and became small. Obviously unwilling to part with the bush, they kind of squeezed into it, as if they were glued…

The daughter of our neighbour, Ilghiza, got ill, " said Zufar's mother with a sigh as she entered the house. She went out in the yard to milk the cow. – The day before yesterday they had the herd's day. She was coming back from pasture and was caught in the rain. The poor girl was soaked to the skin. What's worse, her mother is not at home.

Having heard this news, the heart of Zufar has struck heavily, and his skin has scrawled. What? Neighbour's daughter? Do they mean Gulfiya? It took him a while to realise who his mother was talking about?

" Who are you talking about, mom?"

" About Gulfiya, of course, sonny."

It took Zufar's breath away. As if someone threw down a heavy stone onto his heart, and it felt weighed down under its weight…

Neighbour's daughter... Curly, hazel-eyed Gulfiya. The most beautiful girl on their street, at their school, and even in the entire village. So beautiful and so gentle... Her hazel eyes seem to radiate the divine light and are like a morning dawn! Zufar loves to look at her during the lessons, look into her dreamy eyes, and does not even hear what the teacher is saying .

Ah, these eyes of hers!.. Hazel eyes, which have illuminated the whole world with their light, which has comprised all of the beauty of the universe!..

...Zufar grasped the big cup and stormed out of the house. He was rushing to the backyard, where raspberry bushes were growing.

The sun was already sinking behind the withered horizon. One could hear the old cow, happy with her life, chewing the cud quietly in the cowshed, a young cow sighing loudly after having had a long walk during the day in the herd, and sheep bleating softly...

Zufar spent a long time running back and forth in the raspberry bushes. The berries were falling down, and the remaining small ones were watery and savoury.

The heart of the boy felt squeezed with some strange cold.

Zufar, who has nearly become a Dzhigit, has almost lost hope to collect the good berries, but suddenly he has found what he was looking for – under an apple-tree. The raspberry bushes, having hidden themselves under the tree, grew scrambling over its branches. Having pulled the branches apart, Zufar stopped in surprise: the large berries were filled with juice, ready to fall down. And there are so many snow-white flowers around. Being born by summer heat, they have hidden themselves safely from the breath of the unexpected autumn! It is the apple-tree that saved them in its warm embrace.

Zufar opened the wicket of the Gulfiya's house. In hot weather the wicket was creaking mercilessly, but this time it was silent. Was it because the health of Gulfiya was in jeopardy?

It was quiet in the house. Boxer, such was the name of their tomcat, whose place was on the floor, had fixed himself on a hard chair and was silent. The flowers of geranium, which stood on the windowsills, looked sad.

Then he heard a suppressed moan. Zufar rushed toward it.

In the room with the clean lace curtains on the windows, there laid Gulfiya in the snow-white bed clothes , drowning in the downy pillow and covered by the quilt. The girl looked thin and pale. Her short curls swept the pillow.

She slowly raised her eyelids.

– "How are you, Gulfiya?.. " asked Zufar in a quivered voice.

A-al-ri-ght... " drawled the girl, although it was not so, of course.

" Gulfiya, I have gathered some raspberries for you…"

Where did you get them?.. The rains... have washed away... ours... a long time ago," she said in a low voice.

" Somehow I managed. These berries are not ordinary, but magical ones. They save us from all illnesses. Try them and you will see for yourself. They are of the same colour as your lips when you are healthy."

The girl looked at him as if asking him: can it really be so? She smiled and put one berry to her lips.

That very moment someone entered the house. It was the father of Gulfiya.

Well-well, I thought who that might be, visiting us? So, it's you, buddy," he said approaching his daughter. He put his hand, which smelled of fresh milk, onto her forehead.

Before leaving, Zufar touched her slightly pinked cheeks with his hot lips and said:

Get well. And eat raspberries. By all means…"

Before he finished, her father came in with a cup of hot milk.

Gulfiya followed Zufar with her eyes for a long time from under the heavy eyelids.

In the morning, when the sun was tenderly caressing the pinked up face of Gulfiya, she was already feeling good. Her sparkling brown eyes were completely opened. And her mother was about to come back soon from the city of Kazan, and the weather seemed to be getting better. The girl unfolded the blanket and got up. As she came to the mirror, she saw a fistful of ripe, sweet raspberries that were left after yesterday's visit.

Magical, healing berries!..

# A MEETING

It was a crisp and stormy winter day. Even a dog would not go out in such weather. There was no escape from the cold chilling wind.

Ilham, a Kazan student, having passed his exams with only the excellent marks, set out to his native village. He came to the bus station an hour before the departure of the bus. His luggage, full of empty glass cans, clothes, and some gifts for his relatives, looked huge, but was not at all heavy.

The lad was in a great mood, because, having graduated from school last year, he enrolled at the university he dreamed of, and now, having passed all exams after the New year holidays, he has finally broken free. There were three weeks of vacations waiting for him; a village life. He was missing his father, mother, and little sisters so much.

In the bus, he found himself sitting next to a man of about thirty five years old. They got into conversation. It so happened that Fansyuar, such was the name of his travel companion, graduated from the same university ten years ago and has been working within his specialty. He was travelling to the neighbouring village to visit his mother who was ill.

You, probably, miss your home? " asked Ilham.

" Of course, I do. Can it be any other way, when even the telegraph poles are beckoning you home! answered Fansyuar with the words from a well-known Tatar folk song.

A silence settled for some short time. Only the noise of the bus driving along the road could be heard.

" Do they pay the stipend? " wondered the travel companion.

"They do... I get high grades, but still what I get is just four hundred. I spend half of this amount on a bus pass, and another half is only just enough for one week. The relatives help, but... Well, in short, a student needs up to fifteen hundred a month to live a normal life, " said Ilham.

"Indeed, life is different now. We were happy to have forty or fifty roubles for an easy life... We travelled a lot. What we had was enough even to travel abroad. For example, I visited Tashkent and the Crimea. We had the money, the planes flew several times a day, and air tickets cost not what they cost these days... Did you have an opportunity to visit some other city? I mean a city outside of Tatarstan?"

" No... Not yet..."

" At my time, we were trying hard, studying, striving to learn as much as possible. Now, it seems, everything depends on money, eh?"

Well, in fact, yes, Fansyuar-abziy. If you happen to have failed to pass a test or an exam, you just have to dip into your pocket. Although, if you attended the classes on regular basis, and if you have a clear head, they would not rush to sink you in case you have difficulties. Probably, they have enough of what they want from sons of rich parents."

" Yes, my dear Ilham, the situation with knowledge is really bad these days. Our life is full of ignorance. And the trouble is in the money. Sometimes, it's so hard that you cannot even afford bread..." sighed the travel-companion.

They sat in silence for a while. Meanwhile, the bus was tearing along like mad...

" Ilham, do you live in a hostel?"

" No-o-o... " said the lad drawlingly, as if he wanted to say 'May Allah save me from it!'

" Why?"

" No one wants to live in a hostel nowadays. It is such a hustle-and-bustle there. Absolutely no possibility to study... Drinking, smoking... Hell on earth! It's much better to rent a flat, even though it's expensive. It's better for peace of mind."

" I see. When we were students, everything was in perfect order in hostels. And the girls who lived there were so charming... Ah! I wish I could feast my eyes on them forever! "

Decent girls are but, probably, few in hostels today. Very few, maybe. Most of them drink together with the guys, smoke, and that sort of things... Some dance night after night at discos. No time to study. They come back at five o'clock in the morning to start their classes at eight... And what about finding a job, Fansyuar-abziy, was it difficult? " wondered Ilham.

" No, it was not a problem. People of our profession are always in demand, even today. So, the doors will be open for you, bro. All you need to do is to study. Try hard."

" Really?.."

Ilham wanted to say something else, but his travel-companion interrupted him:

" How do you see your future, I wonder?"

Well, I need to finish my studies first..."

" I understand it. But let's say that you have finished your studies and began working. And your salary is good enough..."

" I would, of course, be doing my job properly. With time, I would have bought myself a flat, a car and would have married."

Alright then, my fellow countryman. It seems that you are not hopeless. Study well and do not live for the day. And what about associate professor Safiullin? Is he still working?"

He is. Still teaching and does not seem to be willing to go, even though he has long been a pensioner."

" Oh, yes. People like him do not surrender their place to the young. I remember him saying that he would retire even when were students. "

...And the bus was still tearing along and along like a mad horse...

" Come think of it, " thought Gulyuzum, an eighty-year-old woman, to herself, having adjusted a hearing device in her ear: " In my time, a person with elementary education would have been considered a scholar, a great mind. We could only dream of studying in a city... The present-day young people are so happy: they can study to their heart's content. They have every opportunity. So many books, so many universities. Choose any, if you have money at hand… You did not experience what we had lived through. Can today's people realise what we had to live with, and what load we had to carry on our shoulders? But it's better that you don't know it."

And still, the bus was tearing along, dashing and rushing, despite the impenetrable snowstorm and foul weather...

# A LETTER

## *(A sad story)*

It was a sad autumn day. The decrepit leaves were falling down from trees. Driven by the wind, they were whirling in the air under the sparse drops of the cold rain and then fell onto the ground. It seemed that they were looking sadly at the sky, regretting: 'Heh, but we did have the happy days', and then they plunged into the sea of dreams...

...At first, she went to the cemetery every day. She wept and wept quietly over the same tomb murmuring something under her breath. Passers-by were staring at her: " What an oddity! She seems to have gone completely mad out of grief" . But there were some who pitied her: " Poor thing, so young. What happened? Who is there, in the tomb?" They were ready to approach her and soothe her, but something prevented them from doing so, and they walked on by.

I live nearby and occasionally walk past this cemetery. Today, again, on this nasty autumn day, she was there, as always, at her usual place, despite the drizzling rain and the bitter cold.

In a simple coat, in a long black skirt, black kerchief and, for some reason, in yellow shoes.

I approached her and asked stumblingly how she felt. The girl peered at me strangely and then, all of a sudden, smiled. However, the mournful expression immediately returned to her face. Maybe because she knew me or felt confident about me (or, most probably, for me to be able to find the answer to my question), she handed over a piece of paper with the words: " Read it, but then return it to me."

At home, I carefully took the paper that was folded into four in my hands. Suddenly, I felt some kind of warmth that ran all over my body… I unfolded it. Yes, it was a letter…

*Hello, my dear! How are you, my beauty?*

*Writing to you is Ilham, who adores you. How are you, my dear? What are you doing? Do you think of me, do you remember me, my sweetheart?*

*The embroidered kerchief, which you have presented to me when sending me off to the army, I keep carefully and carry it in my chest pocket. Though we have been apart for a year, my feelings for you did not grow cold. On the contrary, I love you more than ever!*

*The minutes that I have spent here are like hours, and hours are like days. I've been thinking about you, visualising your tender image in my imagination, and the days pass by faster. It's not easy for you and for me, but, no matter how hard it is for us, let's arm ourselves with patience, my joy. This is how another year of separation will pass quicker. I miss you so much!*

*Do you remember the first time we met?.. I think you do. How can one forget?!*

*…I was walking down the street, and you were returning from the spring-well. Your buckets were full of clear water. I saw you, and my heart gave a leap and began beating fast. I could not understand, how could it be that I had not noticed such a nice, beautiful girl before? How could it be that I was passing her by?! I still see your sky-blue eyes, your red hair, and that mysterious glance and wistful smile of yours. Ever since that very minute I have fallen into the flame of love. The wish to see my love every day and every hour was leading me to where I had met you. When I came to know that you love me too, I was beside myself with happiness! It took me to the seventh heaven! No one could be happier than us! Don't you think?..*

*…I also think of you at night, when I look at the starry sky, and fall asleep in sweet dreams… We meet in my dreams… You are rushing to me in small steps in your light-blue dress that flickers in the wind. 'Ilham, I love you!*

*Love you so much! When will you come back to me, my dear?' – you whisper to me. And I answer: 'Alsu, the bird of my happiness, I, too, love you so much!' No other pair can be happier than us at that moment... Don't you think so?*

*Alright, then. Good bye, my dear. Write letters to me, my love. I will be waiting.*

*Your Ilham, who is completely out of his mind from love for you.*

The next day I gave the letter back to the woman, but did not ask her any questions on how the Dzhigit has died. I did not want to harrow the feelings of the martyr and return her to the world of emotional stress and suffering.

...Many years have passed since that time, but I still remember the tear-stained blue eyes and her sad face. I still have great pity for her. Sometimes I'm looking for her, wishing to soothe her. But... she is no more. Two graves lie next to each other. And two young birches, despite the autumn nasty weather and snowy rain, still stand as if they have come to an agreement, impressing with their beauty, refusing to part with their green attire.

# A TITMOUSE

A room in a hostel where Sarah lives. The unsmiling October sun looks into the window. It skews through the branches of the tall birches that put on the yellow dresses, but their beauty does not touch the sun. It is sparing of communication and does not hurry to yield itself to emotions. It is s either hiding them or, maybe, the accumulated sorrows do not allow it to open up? There is a flame blazing inside it, but outside the sun looks as if nothing is happening... Come guess what is on its mind...

The sun is shining, but it's cold in the street. It's warm in the room, but if you show your face outside, the autumn wind will immediately attempt to give your nose a tweak.

The view from the window is amazing: the aspens have almost shed their leaves. Just a few lonesome leaves were throbbing in the wind. The leaves of maple trees are still contesting with the autumn winds, not yielding to them, still staying in their places, although they have dried up and shrunk a little. Their wish to live is clearly strong. Only the birches are not in hurry to take off their gorgeous yellow coats. All cannot have such an elegant beauty. The green attire of a birch is beautiful, but the yellow one is good in its way too. The latter involuntarily attracts the delighted looks, transforming in the sunrays into the sheer gold. The eyes hurt to look at such splendour.

The middle of October. The autumn rules all around.

Sarah was alone. Her roommates went to a library in the morning to study, but she stayed. She did not feel like going anywhere. Something was holding her at home, some premonition was oppressing her.

Looking at the jaded birches, she thought of many things, having plunged into the golden environment of autumn. Her look sank in the yellowed leaves, and her thoughts were swallowed up by the autumn sadness.

...Some curious humstrum distracted her. Sarah startled and, having forced her eyes from the leaves, began looking around for the performer. Here it is. It's a small titmouse that landed on the outside of the window frame. Having seen the little bird, the girl calmed down. Their eyes met. Both the titmouse and the girl were looking at each other, fearing to move.

Sarah feels strange: she saw in the look of the little bird some understandable sadness, warmth, and even love. But where did she see the same sad black eyes?.. They are so close to her, so dear... The girl was afraid that the little bird would fly up and disappear forever in the expanse of the blue sky...

Hello, little bird! You must be hungry? " asked Sarah, having recollected herself. She crumbed the table, opened the vent pane and stuck her hand out of the window. At first, the titmouse got embarrassed and, as if having scented a catch, flew over to a branch of a birch. " Come on! Come here, dear! You surely want to eat. It's so cold now. Very, very cold, " coo ed Sarah.

The little bird fluttered to the other branch, the tender voice of the girl has calmed it down. Suddenly the titmouse fluttered to the girl's hand, snatched a crumb that looked heavier, and then flew off to the top of the tree. This repeated several times. Sarah was watching it, holding her breath, fearing to frighten it... The titmouse surprised Sarah: it flew off the branch again and fluttered to the girl's hand. Did it want to thank her? Their eyes met again, and the girl felt the same feeling of warmth and closeness... The bird cried something and soared up into the blue sky. It was rising higher and higher, becoming smaller and smaller. Then it turned into a hardly visible point... And then disappeared completely...

Sarah felt sad. She kept on looking in the little bird's direction. It seemed that the little titmouse would return and soothe her... Its farewell cry was still ringing in her ears. And the eyes...

Indeed, the eyes of the little bird had it all – sadness, so familiar to Sarah, closeness and warmth, so understandable, and the look, so full of love. But where did she see it? In whose black and sad eyes?.. They are so close, so dear to her...

...Suddenly, the heart of Sarah squeezed, her eyes dimmed, tears welled from her eyes, in which there has just recently stood the question that troubled her, and her heart has kind of took off:

" Ra-a-a-mi-i-il! My lo-o-o-o-ve!.." The sorrowful, bloodcurdling c ry of the girl has struck and woken up the city that was wrapped up in the eternal fuss and petty troubles, and has brought it to senses for an instant.

...A feather of the small bird that was brought by the wind from somewhere floated in the air, flying first to the left, then to the right and then fell right on the moist lips of Sarah.

Yes, she recognised in the titmouse her first and probably her last love, who died tragically in the plane crash last year. They say that the souls of those who went to the next world sometimes return to the living and to those who are dear to them...

# THE SOUL

Something strange has begun happening to my soul. Before that day it was kind of enchained by ice. Then it suddenly began stirring like a butterfly that unexpectedly felt the warmth of sun rays in the middle of winter. Soon it has started moving, having thrown off the ice crust, and flapped its wings by the snow-covered window, through which entering the dim room was the poor dull light. Some wonderful warm breath has awakened it from its sleep and blown up the sparks of life in it. The soul hurried to liven up the beautiful spring days that were snoozing somewhere before their time, to hasten them.

So, what has happened to my soul? It kind of feels the mysterious force, the magic gesture. It hurries to break the icy glass and break free... But it's blistering cold outside, chilling to the bone. Don't know why I woke up? I can't understand it either. It seems to me that I will only be able to find the answer outside the window. It's only there where everything will become clear...

Having found a tiny back door, my soul, like a butterfly that strives for freedom, thirsting for a gulp of fresh air, broke loose, rushed into the embrace of the cold winter, but did not fall. It flew over the ground and, finally, brought spring with it, shared generously the warmth with the whole world, having scattered and disseminated it all over. Then it transformed into the rustle of leaves on the green trees that were covered by white flowers, into the unceasing chatter of birds, and then dissolved among the tender sunrays, having turned into the spring breeze. It became a one-eyed narcissus, a sweet-voiced nightingale that sings an eternal song of love . What a blessing! Ah, what a joy! The soul gave itself to the mysterious force of magic feelings... But what is it?.. What?..

...Well, yes, yes, only the almighty, pure love is capable of doing such miracles. It's only it that can bring the eternal spring with it! That's only it...

# ONE SONG WILL BE ENOUGH

*Yesterday I heard: someone was singing...*
G. Tukay

Half past eleven p.m. A student hostel is preparing for sleep. It's only me and my friend who are not willing to go to bed; we sat down to make an abstract of the assignment. The small ventilation window was open.

Suddenly, someone began blowing the bellows of an accordion. I shivered with surprise... And then the melody of the well-known song " Kubalyaghem" (" Oh, My Butterfly" ) began flowing! Something has happened to my soul. The accordion player, a young lad, began singing in a crisp voice:

*What id a butterfly would land onto a flower,*
*Would it sway?..*

The native, Tatar song, the folk melody, has begun. It was so strange to hear it, since my soul has already got accustomed to the fact that people in cities are indifferent to our songs. Indeed, who would have thought that here, where Russian speech was heard more frequently, someone would be singing a Tatar song in the middle of the night to the accompaniment of an accordion?! One cannot meet such things today even in the Tatar villages...

*...At the foot of the hill, at the foot of the hill*
*There is a round, frozen spring-well...*

Great!.. So good!.. The heart got filled with happiness and sadness, with the light and warmth of the familiar melody... Involuntary tears were welling in my eyes.

*...The moths are plenty in the world,*

*But brave ones can hardly be found...*

I wanted to run out to see who was singing. Because it was our, native, Tatar song!.. I imagined a village, its half-empty streets that have not heard an accordion for a long time... Heigh ho! It's such a pity that I cannot play an accordion, for I would have shown them all! And our sleepy village that lost its former spiritual force would awake at once!

...I came to the window... The song subsided...

And then, suddenly, a young, ringing, innocent girl's voice shouted to the whole world:

I love you!"

What is it?.. The return of the past?.. A mess of times and centuries?.. Or the excitement, the feelings, hidden deep down inside, that suddenly broke out?..

Oh, yes, such things do happen. The feelings wake up sometimes and touch the dusty strings of the soul to bring it back to life. It proved that one Tatar song was enough for that. Oh!..

# INTERVIEWS

# YULDUZ KHALIULLIN:
# " DIPLOMATS CAN GIVE A HEAD START TO SECRET SERVICE MEN! "

*We communicate much with a famous diplomat, scientist and publicist Yulduz Khaliullin, who lives in Moscow, but, unfortunately, now we have to talk more often only by phone. He is an orientalist by education, a diplomat by profession, and a writer, scientist and publicist by his state of mind. He is an author of two dozen books and hundreds of articles on a variety of topics. He is a Doctor of Economics, corresponding member of the International Economic Academy of Eurasia. In addition to his mother tongue Tatar and Russian languages, he is fluent in many languages that are not quite so simple.*

*Yulduz Nurievich was born in 1936 in the village of Iske Kyzyl-Yar (literally translated: Old Krasny Yar) of the Agryz district of the Republic of Tatarstan. About forty years of his life were connected with embassies of the USSR and the Russian Federation in Indonesia, Pakistan, Romania, Nepal, Maldives, Sri Lanka, Kyrgyzstan, Kazakhstan, he was engaged in scientific and writing activities for more than twenty years. His book ' Nobel Prize Winner Abdus Salam', dedicated to an outstanding physicist, professor at the University of London, was published five times in Russian and English.*

*In his ninth decade of life, Yulduz Nurievich is full of energy and creative plans. His stories about the events of the past, reflections on international diplomacy, problems of education, science and culture are of great interest. However, the reader will fully get acquainted with his life and work in this interview.*

*– Yulduz-aby, how did a simple village boy get a desire to enter the Moscow State Institute of International Relations? And then you also graduated from the Diplomatic Academy and its postgraduate program…*

– I was eager to learn foreign languages since childhood. Perhaps my childhood spent next to my grandmother had an impact. Granny Fakhernisa performed five prayers daily, she knew verses from the Quran by heart. It was then that a desire arose in my soul to study Arabic and translate these verses into Tatar for her.

I heard about MGIMO as a closed educational institution belonging to the Ministry of Foreign Affairs of the USSR while serving in the army. In May 1958, a meeting of the secretaries of Komsomol organizations of military units was held in Rostov-on-Don. One of the heads of the political department of the military district spoke there. He said that the military personnel, whose term of service ends this year, have the opportunity to pass the entrance exams to MGIMO, and the political department can give recommendations to them. They were equal to recommendations of the regional Committee of the CPSU. Further, the colonel from the political department said that those who showed interest in this would have to pass a small preliminary language exam. This was unusual for me, since almost none of us had ever heard of the existence of such an institution.

Thirty people took part in the preliminary exam, of which three were chosen. In the English language group my friend Alexander Rhud turned out to be the strongest, Levin passed the test in French. And I was the best in the German language group.

Back in the unit I reported to my commander Viktor Fedorovich Ivanov about the results and asked his opinion about MGIMO. He said, " This is exactly the direction you need to go. I am sure that you will succeed" .

At the end of June the three of us, Rhud, Levin and I, went to Moscow. Unlike my comrades, I was going to the capital for the first time. Having scored seventeen points out of twenty, I passed the competition, but my friends could not... That year there was an unprecedented competition: eighteen people for a vacancy, and every third, like us, in a military uniform.

*– Yulduz-aby, what foreign languages do you know? What language was the most difficult to learn? Are you using them now?*

– I know Urdu. It is the first official language in Pakistan. Later I studied Hindi. It is the official language of India. I also mastered English, which was necessary for conducting everyday work. I can speak German, French, Turkish, as well as Indonesian.

Learning languages is not easy. Urdu uses the Arabic alphabet. The Arabic alphabet consists of twenty-eight letters, then additional new letters are added here. This means that the language becomes even more difficult. When young, everything was studied with great interest...

I use them when necessary, but gradually I am forgetting some words. I remember Urdu well, and sometimes I speak Hindi. I didn't have to speak Indonesian anymore, but I advised my student, Eduard Gayazovich Islamov, a resident of Naberezhnye Chelny, to learn this wonderful language. He has mastered Indonesian and Malaysian languages. The difference between them is small. Edward studied the economy of Malaysia. I supervised his thesis. Then he developed this topic, defended his dissertation, became a Doctor of Economics and published a book.

*– You started your career in Indonesia, and during your work there have been serious changes, historical upheavals. They killed communists, put them to prison... Wasn't it scary? After all, the Soviet Union was a large communist state, and you are a representative of this country.*

– When the war against the communists began in 1965, we diplomats had to work with great difficulty. I remember a significant event. During the reign of the first President Sukarno (1901-1970), the chairman of the Central Committee of the Communist Party of the country Dipa Nusantara Aidit (1923-1965) was a minister in the government. Relations between our country and Indonesia were good, in the evenings we held youth parties in Jakarta.

At one of these parties, when the orchestra started playing, everyone parted, freeing up the center. The dance began, which lasted for about half an hour. During this time I managed to meet and talk with a group of Jakarta young men, they called themselves activists of the Communist Youth Union of Indonesia. They were interested in what specialties they teach at Moscow State University. The orchestra stopped, and the young men around me almost simultaneously bowing their heads, took two steps back, giving way to a young Indonesian who was dancing with my wife. The dance lasted for about fifteen minutes.

After exchanging pleasantries I started a conversation with him. The Indonesian wanted to know more about us, and he started asking: "You are probably representatives of one of the Central Asian republics of the Soviet Union, aren't you?" I said: " No, we are Muscovites, Tatars by nationality…" and told him what we were and what kind of people we were. After a long conversation he left.

Then we moved to another hall, where the ceremony of the feast began. Boris Golovanov, our ambassador's translator, came up and asked me with a smile: " Do you know who your wife danced with?" " No", I said, " but he is an exceptionally pleasant, intelligent Indonesian. But why?.." " This is the chairman of the Central Committee of the Communist Party of Indonesia, Aidit…" – concluded B. Golovanov significantly.

When Aidit, who was the head of the Communist Party of Indonesia for almost twenty years, was killed, we mourned him. He was only 42 years old. There was a military coup. About a million communists were killed. President Sukarno was not touched, but he had to live in his house under guard and died a few years later.

*— You met the collapse of the USSR as temporary charge d'affaires of the USSR in the Kingdom of Nepal. What did you feel watching this historical upheaval of the global significance from the sidelines?*

— I had to watch the disappearance of the once powerful country from the political map of the world from the ' roof of the world' with heavy feelings, with pain in my heart. It was at this time that the Communist Party of Nepal won the elections. We often talked with the chairman of the party, Man Mohan Adhikari (1920-1999). These days our meetings have become even more frequent. The main question haunted him: " What obscure changes are taking place in the USSR? What will be the result of these changes?"

The essence of my concern was something else: to prevent deterioration of bilateral relations, to preserve their friendly character accumulated over decades of cooperation. At all costs it was necessary to avoid the internal political crisis and the inevitable collapse of the USSR alienating the Nepalese leadership from our country – from Russia as it often happens at such critical moments in history. This is how I understood my main task as an envoy of my country, which was rapidly and irretrievably losing its positions on the international stage at that time.

*— Yulduz-aby, have you ever had a desire to stay there while working abroad?*

— I have never had such a desire. Never. No matter who and no matter how big a person you are, there is nothing more precious than your country. Those who left once still come back. Actor Mikhail Kozakov, for example, the famous cellist Mstislav Rostropovich, his wife, the famous opera singer Galina Vishnevskaya and others. They say Boris Berezovsky had such a desire too. The soul of any person is connected with the motherland by invisible threads. The connection with the motherland can never be broken forever.

*– You admitted that you love poetry, especially the works of George Byron. Why such a love for literature? I would like to hear your opinion about poetry...*

– In my opinion, if there were no Byron, there would be no Pushkin and Lermontov. Byron was their teacher. Via these classics of Russian poetry, the great English poet influenced the great Tatar poet Gabdulla Tukay. It is interesting that Byron's first poem was translated into Russian in 1815, and until today about 300 translators have repeatedly translated his works. Among them there are such great poets as Vasily Zhukovsky, Mikhail Lermontov, Samuel Marshak, Boris Pasternak. The new word in the world of poetry, the beauty and grandeur of Byron's works influenced greatly his followers and creative people in general!

Since we touched on poetry, here is another thing I want to say. First of all, it is not only poets who make themselves poets, but excellent translators too. Omar Khayyam, for example. Edward Fitzgerald, famous English poet of the XIX century (1809–1883) devoted the whole of his life to translating his poems into English. Thanks to Fitzgerald, the poems and poetry of the Persian poet have received worldwide recognition. Secondly, why Omar Khayyam? In addition to being known as a poet, he was also an outstanding scientist and mathematician. The most famous mathematician of the Muslim world. He was among the first ones to discover algebraic geometry that appeared in Europe only centuries later. In the XI century Omar Khayyam created a solar calendar. It turned out to be much more accurate than the Gregorian calendar that began to be used in the West 500 years later.

From my understanding of Omar Khayyam as a scientist, mathematician and poet I came to the conclusion that people of a technical mindset can make many interesting and new discoveries in poetry.

The second example of this kind is Ravil Bukharaev. I had a chance to communicate with him for ten years. He graduated from the faculty of mechanics and mathematics of Kazan State University, postgraduate training program in theoretical cybernetics at Moscow State University. Despite the fact that he was a ready-made doctor of science, he did not go this direction, but chose literature or rather poetry. Imagine: during the Soviet Union he was on a business trip to Hungary for about a year and a half and began writing poems in Hungarian. They were printed in the periodicals. And Hungarian is one of the most difficult languages in Europe. I don't think he studied the language very well and clearly, but as a cyberneticist he fished out poetic words and sentences that make it possible to express his thoughts philosophically.

I compare Omar Khayyam and Ravil Bukharayev, who were both mathematicians and poets. My reflections on this led me to the conclusion that the world culture, including Russian, is divided into two categories. They run parallel to each other. The first category is created by humanitarians. This includes writers, artists and politicians. The second, more convincing culture is created by specialists of natural sciences: physicists, mathematicians, biologists, chemists… These two groups don't really communicate with each other, because their understanding of the world is different. Recently, the people born to combine both categories and connect these parallels are rare.

*— In a short period of time your book about Abdus Salam has been published five times: in 2006, 2008, 2016, 2017 – in Russian in Moscow and Kazan; in 2010 – in English in Dubna at the publishing house of the Joint Institute for Nuclear Research. In 2010 the book was presented at Imperial College of London, in 2011 – in New York, Philadelphia and Washington (at the Library of the USA Congress).*

### *How did the desire to write a book arise?*

   – It started very unusually, sometimes completely random phenomena push a person in a completely different direction.

   This happened in 1967-1968. I was assigned to accompany a parliamentary delegation that flew from the Soviet Union to Pakistan. We were supposed to go from Karachi to Lahore and then to Islamabad. So we stopped in Lahore and stayed there for a day. The local government received us very warmly and arranged a formal reception. And at the reception an outstanding Pakistani poet, winner of the Lenin Peace Prize, my friend Ahmad Faiz came up to me and said: " Let's go to an interesting place" . I ask him " Where to? Quit the reception, leave my delegates?!" To which he replied: " There's nothing wrong with that. Professor Abdus Salam is currently speaking in quantum physics at the Punjab University" . " I don't know much about quantum physics" . – " And I don't know it at all, but it's interesting to listen to him" .

   After all, the two of us ' ran away' from the reception. I asked the Pakistanis to escort my delegation to the hotel without telling them where I was going.

   After listening to a part of the speech Ahmad Faiz told me: " Let me introduce you to Abdus Salam" . I told him: " It's awkward. We have to leave Lahore for Islamabad in two hours" .

   I went back to my delegates, and they attacked me: " You abandoned us. We will inform the ambassador about you…" I said " Please do" . I had already prepared the information that Abdus Salam was an outstanding physicist of Pakistan, that he should be enlisted to the USSR Academy of Sciences as a foreign member. The ambassador liked this idea, he immediately signed the information and it was sent to Moscow. My proposal coincided with the opinion of academician Bogolyubov. Thus, in 1971, eight years before winning the Nobel Prize, Abdus Salam was enlisted to the USSR Academy of Sciences.

At that time Abdus Salam held the high post of chief scientific adviser to the President of Pakistan Ayub Khan, specially established for him, and regularly visited his homeland on the way from London, and his speeches were willingly printed in newspapers and magazines.

When we went back to Moscow, the head of the South Asia Department of the USSR Ministry of Foreign Affairs A. Fomin told me that " these materials about Abdus Salam were very useful" for the administration of the USSR Academy of Sciences when the issue of electing a scientist as a foreign member was being decided there.

Then all this was forgotten, there was no time to think about it. After Pakistan I worked in Romania, then in Nepal, etc. And when I retired, my wife told me: " I accidentally found your old papers, Pakistani newspapers, some kind of certificates. Please take a look, maybe you need them, you can find something interesting there" .

I started looking through the papers and found my information about Abdus Salam. I quickly wrote two articles and sent them to a Moscow newspaper and the glamorous magazine " Persona" . I did not have to wait long. The article published in " Persona" happened to be next to the article of the famous physicist Sergei Petrovich Kapitsa. He, a Doctor of Physics and Mathematics, writes about demography, me, a humanitarian - about the contribution of Abdus Salam to physics. It was very nice.

Then I translated this article into English and sent it to Imperial College of London, at the same time I asked for additional materials on the topic under study. Abdus Salam was a head of the Department of theoretical physics there for about forty years.

I received an unexpected response from London: an invitation to work in libraries and archives. So in the early summer of 2005, for the first time I found myself in the capital of the British Empire, in the former colonies of which (Pakistan, Sri Lanka, Nepal) I worked for about fifteen years.

In the famous reading room of the British Museum I took a copy of the extensive article about Abdus Salam from the just-published multi-volume edition of Oxford National Biography with information about famous people from British subjects only. It was a peculiar discovery, as far as Abdus Salam always remained a citizen of Pakistan, he never accepted citizenship of other countries. There were creative disappointments as well. As it turned out, the main archive of the scientist is not in London, but in Trieste, where professor Abdus Salam headed the Scientific center for theoretical physics created by him for thirty years.

There was also a pleasant surprise waiting for me in London, which I could not have dreamed of. Thanks to the kind assistance of the greatest theologian of the modern Muslim world Hazrat Mirza Masrur Ahmad I got acquainted with the close relatives of professor Abdus Salam living in England. By the invitation of the scientist's elder son Ahmad Salam I visited the house of the great physicist in the Putney district in south-west London, where he lived for many years. The younger son Omar Salam, who followed his father's path, walked me around Cambridge University, where the great physicist began his scientific career once and where his son lectures higher mathematics.

I also got acquainted with the archive of Abdus Salam at the International scientific center for theoretical physics in Trieste, and visited the library there. Thus, the life of an outstanding Muslim scientist led me to quantum physics.

Back in Moscow I wrote a book in a month. The first edition of " Nobel prize winner Abdus Salam" was published in Moscow, the second – in the Academy of Sciences of the Republic of Tatarstan, and then the book was translated into English. Presentations were held in Moscow, Kazan, London... In the UK the presentation was held at Imperial College, in office No. 521, where the scientist worked all his life. Then the book in English was presented at Oxford University, at the Library of

Congress of the USA and in other cities and countries.

Studying Abdus Salam's life has confirmed in my opinion that people with technical and scientific thinking see the world much stronger and with greater understanding. This is a strong parallel culture, even politics.

— *How fast and effective was the transition from diplomacy to the problems of quantum physics, global oceans and the Arctic, climate change?*

— It happened very quickly. I was forced to study quantum physics after retirement. My wife works, I stay at home, write books, and articles . I enjoy studying Albert Einstein's theory of relativity and quantum physics. These are such complicated things, sometimes I don't understand them at all. This is why they are so attractive. Inaccessible, incomprehensible things always seem interesting.

I will give an example. The English writer Rudyard Kipling sets off from India on a long journey by steamer to meet the American novelist Mark Twain. Finally, he arrives on another continent. They met and started talking, and he asks Mark Twain: " What are you doing now?" " I have just read a very interesting article in the encyclopedia on mathematics. The specialist writes. Of course, I understood nothing, but it's written beautifully. It is important that it is beautifully written, and it can be interpreted in different ways" , the other one replies.

If quantum and nuclear physicists and scientists have not found any lapses in my book about Abdus Salam, then this is normal. In this case, it is not necessary to go too deep.

— *Based on your experience, how difficult and responsible was the work of a diplomat before and what is it like in the current era of change?*

— If diplomats skillfully work with foreign representatives, love this country, study it with interest, then sometimes they can give a head start to intelligence officers, even illegal intelligence officers. But not everyone does it. It is necessary to know the language, history, mentality of the people of the country where you work, meet them often and talk to them.

In the autumn of 1967 in the Pakistani city of Mirpur Khas, I took part in the ' mushaira' (a competition of amateur poets on a given topic). The competition was not easy. The subject was announced (for example, autumn) to which in a short period of time one has to compose a poem in three or four stanzas and recite it. The competition was held in Urdu! About twenty people participated there. Unexpectedly to myself, I reached the final, but lost to a cute zamindar of Baluchi origin about forty years old. When he found out that his opponent was a Soviet vice–consul with a Muslim surname, he invited me to lunch at his ancestral estate. In a huge mango garden we drank several glasses of French Bordeaux at the dining table, to Soviet-Pakistani friendship. In such a romantic atmosphere my acquaintance with Mir Ghaus Baksh Talpur, a large landowner of Mirpur Khas district, took place.

Talpur told me many different stories from the life of his ancestors. For two centuries, the Talpurs ruled the province of Sindh absolutely. They were genetically related to militant Baluchi tribes from the mountain areas, that is, newcomers to the local Sindh population. The last Talpur principality in Khairpur was ' dismissed' only in 1955. The descendants of the Talpurs retained large areas of land throughout the province; they were hunted by many political parties, especially during election campaigns. Dozens of representatives of the top of the clan were members of the government of Sindh province in recent times .

At the ' narrow' dinners in the residence of Mir Ghaus Baksh Talpur in Karachi, very peculiar people gathered – the cream of the Pakistani society of that time. There, for example, I met Akbar Bugti, the future governor of Baluchistan, who in 1974 accompanied Z. A. Bhutto during his official visit to the USSR.

Surprisingly, Talpur's close friends gradually became our family friends. Among them, the big Punjabi entrepreneurs, the brothers Rafiq, Shafiq and Tawfiq, owners of several family factories in Karachi, closely connected with government orders, deserve special mention. My wife and I often went to their family dinners.

Once Talpur addressed me with an unusual request. During the conversation, it turned out that the leaders of the Muslim League and the Democratic Party offered him to take part in the parliamentary elections upcoming soon. " Mr. Khaliullin, you know the political situation well, from which party should I nominate my candidacy?" – he asked.

My answer was sincere and sharp: " I consider, neither of the two parties will be able to win the elections. They are outdated already, they have different principles already. If possible, you should nominate your candidacy from the new Pakistan People's Party of Zulfikar Ali Bhutto. Young people will vote for this party" .

Initially, Bhutto occupied the position of foreign minister, and after criticizing the policies of president Mohammad Ayub Khan, he resigned and established his own oppositional " Pakistan People's Party" .

A couple of weeks later, Talpur took me to Bhutto's residence. A dinner was organized there on the occasion of the final approval of the party list of candidates for the upcoming elections. The future political force has gathered. All of them are sitting at the table, giving toasts but speaking English. It is soon my turn, and I'm very worried...

Thus, after a few glasses of whiskey, it was my turn to make a toast – unlike others who spoke English – I read an eight-line verse in Urdu, composed in anticipation of my word, where Bhutto's name was mentioned twice in the elegant Persian isafet construction " Wazir-e-Azem mustaqbil" , which means " future prime minister" .

Bhutto reacted to this instantly: " Oh, how beautifully you talk! If my party is successful in the elections, and I have no doubt about it, I invite you to the post of Minister of Culture. And you will probably have to start with Urdu literature lessons for my ministers, perhaps for me" , he added after a short pause.

Everyone laughed together, because they knew well that Bhutto was a brilliant speaker in English and Sindhi, but for some reason avoided speaking Urdu– the official language of Pakistan. A little later, a year after coming to power, he began to speak to the people Urdu with the same success. And at the time of our meeting, he was only the leader of the opposition, aspiring to power.

Then everyone cast a puzzled glance in my direction: where, they say, did this unknown candidate for the ministerial post come from. My friend Talpur was forced to intervene in the conversation: "Unfortunately, this is not possible, sir. Poet Khaliullah is not a citizen of Pakistan, although he is fond of your political views, but he holds the post of vice consul of the USSR Consulate General in Karachi" , he said. " Then I invite him as the ambassador of the USSR at my future government" , Bhutto said, not embarrassed at all.

Later at this party I had a half-hour conversation with Z. A. Bhutto vis-a-vis, where he clearly outlined the political situation in the country and the prospects for the development of events around Pakistan. I informed the center and the embassy about this: I received thanks from the USSR Foreign Ministry for interesting and timely information and at the same time a reprimand from Ambassador M. Degtyar for an unauthorized meeting with the opposition leader.

Two years later, in November 1972, I returned to Karachi as a consul and right at the exit from the airport I came face to face with M. G. B. Talpur. He was in a hurry to board a plane for Islamabad. Talpur hugged me and, smiling broadly, thanked me for the conversation that took place two years ago: " Your political instinct turned out to be unmistakable – my brother and I became deputies of the parliament from the now ruling party of Z. A. Bhutto " .

Thus, during the next four years of work in Pakistan (1972-1976), regular communication with the Talpurs gave me the opportunity to be aware of the activities of the Bhutto government, about the main trends of Pakistan's foreign and domestic policy, because my friend zamindar M. G. B. Talpour was one of the leaders of the parliamentary faction of the ruling party, and his elder brother Mir Ali Ahmad Talpour was the Minister of Defense.

*– Yulduz-aby, we all know what is happening in the world today. What do you think the world wants today? Are there ways out of crises? Or does humanity simply lack traditional diplomacy?*

– Of course, what is happening in the Middle East is tragic. In no case should one interfere in the affairs of other countries and participate in their home political affairs. In my opinion, both Americans and Europeans have understood something, understood what is happening in Libya, Syria, Iraq. There were American troops in Iraq for several years, after their departure the country returned to the crisis again. There is no result, the same internal war is going on. The situation is similar in Afghanistan.

My opinion is this: there should be a good, skillfully managed dictatorship in developing countries at some point, because the society of many developing countries is not yet ready for full-fledged democracy. Democracy is beginning to be used by certain forces in their own interests, as a result differences are obtained.

The largest democracy in the Third World is in India. As a result of direct elections the Government often changes. The army does not interfere in internal affairs and certain leaders come democratically. What is India? It is a nuclear-armed power with a population of 1.3 billion people. Whoever comes to power there, the laws will not change, development will continue.

Ukraine is not an easy task. Both for us and for them. Ukraine is being dragged to the side of the West. And Ukraine, both on national principles and on history, especially on the economy, is very strongly connected with Russia. Many products produced by Ukraine do not correspond to Europe in quality, but they were suitable for Russia.

Ukraine should not throw its army against its own people and blame Russia for everything. They say that history does not know the subjunctive mood.

*– In recent years, Kazan has come to the forefront of the world fame. Which way should it and its republic go further in the conditions of globalization? What is the future of the Tatar people to you opinion?*

– It is often said that Kazan is the third capital of Russia after Moscow and St. Petersburg. True, Nizhny Novgorod and Yekaterinburg also make a claim for this, but these are only hypothetical expressions. Indeed, Kazan was able to prove itself in the new conditions of the Russian Federation and actively continues this work in many areas. All-Russian and international conferences, meetings, summits, competitions are often held here. And guests enjoy hospitality of Kazan with pleasure.

" Will the Tatar language survive until the middle of the century?" – I am concerned about this issue. Scientific terminology of the Tatar language has not been developed. Who will be able to study quantum physics with the knowledge of the 11th grade of the Tatar language? And IT technologies? Now Russians also use English terminology. 70-80% of all information is in English. You can't do anything, there should be a completely different approach.

It is necessary to educate the Tatar elite. A modern elite that speaks three languages – Tatar, Russian, English. It is necessary to prepare not only the political, but also the economic , cultural elite.

In the XIX – early XX century, the Tatars had special elite schools – madrasas . In our Agryz district, for example, it is " Izh-Bubi" madrasah from which many advanced people came out in their time . In my opinion, only with a good knowledge of the mother tongue, history, culture, awareness of one's nationality, one can survive and continue development.

You can't blame the modern young people, they study IT technologies in English and Russian. In this area, it would be possible to find a place for the Tatar language. It is necessary to create conditions for full-fledged study of the mother tongue, for communication in the mother tongue and to lead the way.

# MUSA CHAKHOROVSKY:
## "LET'S BE ONE BIG FAMILY"

*Tatar poet, translator, journalist and publisher Musa Chakharkhan Chakhorovsky successfully works in the city of Wroclaw in Poland. He translated into Polish the works of G. Tukay, M. Jalil, modern Tatar writers A. Mushinsky, L. Shaekh. In turn, the poems and prose of our compatriots were printed in our city of Kazan in Tatar and Russian.*

*Musa Chakhorovsky was born in 1953 in Wroclaw, in a family of Polish Tatars. He served in the army, worked as a war correspondent. After being discharged into the reserve, he began to actively cooperate in Polish public Tatar-Muslim organizations. He was editor-in-chief of magazines ' As–Salam' and ' Muzułmanie Rzeczypospolitej' (' Muslims of the Polish Republic'), deputy editor-in-chief of the ' Tatar Life' magazine... Since 2009 he has been editor-in-chief of the ' Przegląd Tatarski' quarterly edition (' Tatar Review' ) and since 2014 the leading editor of ' Rocznik Tatarów Polskich' (' Yearbook of Polish Tatars' ). In addition, Musa Chakhorovsky served as the head of the press service of the Muslim Religious Union in the Republic of Poland.*

*His poetic debut took place in 1973. Since then, his poems have appeared in many Polish literary and cultural magazines, as well as in the Tatar press of Poland (' Rocznik Tatarów Polskich', ' Życie Tatarskie', ' Przegląd Tatarski' ), in the periodical of Lithuanian Tatars 'Lietuvos totoriai' (' Tatars of Lithuania' ), in the journal ' AlTaBaş' (' AlTaBash' ), which is published by the Tatar-Bashkir community in Germany. His poem dedicated to the Tatar people is* included in the Polish language textbook for the 6th grade. Chakhorovsky's poems have been published in 16 personal poetry collections (including - alongside with Tatar poets of Poland and Lithuania – Selim Khazbievich and Adas Yakubauskas). In 2021 his prose appeared in ' Tatarskie serca' (' Tatar Hearts' ) collection next to the stories of modern Tatar authors that he translated into Polish.

In 2018 Musa Chakhorovsky published the Quran in its original translation, as well as three collections of Tatar folk tales together with his son Daniel.

Musa Chakhorovsky is a complex creative personality. The vital heritage of ancient ancestors is felt In his poetry and prose – the boundless steppe, the tread of fleet-footed Argamak horses, the whistling of arrows and the smell of fragrant smoke curling from a felt yurt high into the sky...

**– Musa-aby, I think many people know about the ancient historical relationship between Tatars and Poles, so let's start right away with your ancestral roots.**

– Indeed, the first Polish-Tatar contacts (although perhaps not so much Tatar as Mongolian) date back to the reign of Batu Khan in the first half of the XIII century. Then for centuries Poland had close ties with the Tatars, especially with the Crimean and Kazan khanates, as well as with Turkey, Persia and Azerbaijan. Tens of thousands or even more Turks from the Russian Empire and the former USSR settled in Poland. As a result, as they say today, about two million Poles can say that they are of Turkic origin.

My father's Tatar blood goes back to the XIV century. It was then that Princess Anna Danuta, a daughter of Grand Duke Keistut of Lithuania, was to marry Prince Janusz of Mazovia. In her retinue there was a detachment of Tatar warriors who later lived not far from the princely stronghold. One of these Tatar warriors was to become our ancestor, who, like his other companions, remained on this land forever.

My family comes from the small Mazovian nobility of the tiny village of Chakhorovo. Maybe my ancestor's name was Chakhar (Jakhar), maybe he was from Chakhar ulus?

My mother's ancestors, Tatars, come from prisoners of war who arrived in Poland after the Vienna campaign of King Jan III Sobieski in 1683. They were settled on the so–called royal lands of Greater Poland, including the vicinity of the village of Wapno, and quickly dissolved among the local population. Anyway, as I remember myself, I knew that I am different from the people around me, that I am of Tatar blood.

**– What are your parents and what was your childhood like?**

– My paternal grandfather Alexander served in the Tsarist army, he was a sub-officer of the 90th Onega Regiment. He participated in the First World War and then in the Polish-Bolshevik War. He was a cavalryman and was wounded in one of the battles.

My father Daniel served in the Polish army in 1946-1980. I also served in the army in 1973-1995. I was a military journalist, editor of the newspaper of the Silesian military district.

All this made my childhood military. I was born in a military hospital, where my sons were born too. We lived very close to the barracks. A lot of events for children were organized in the military unit – Christmas parties, children's days... The army organized summer camps for children and family vacations. Our neighbors were army people, my friends were from military families. My elementary school was named after the First Army of the Polish Armed Forces...

My mom was a housekeeper and looked after my sister and me. My sister (two years older than me) married an army man later.

**– When and at what age did you start your career? And more: how did you combine poetry with journalism?**

– My career began when I was 16–17 years old. My colleagues were not interested in poetry, and I had no one to talk to about it. The real poets seemed to be divine people, inaccessible to people like me.

And I made my debut in the wall newspaper of the technical school, where they put one of my poems. But I was also interested in journalistic work, the opportunity to meet different people, talk to them, and then describe their lives and problems. It was then that I began to realize the importance of words, their accuracy, imagery and power.

It is very difficult to combine journalism with poetry. Both of them, it would seem, are different branches of the verbal art, on the other hand, they equally demand truth and honesty. Both a journalist and a poet should do their job not only with their minds, but also with their hearts. I understood this and did my best... but at some point I had to make a choice...

**– The translation is also your creative activity. But translation of works of literature and the Quran are two different things. How did you come up with the idea of translating the Holy Book of Muslims? Has anyone translated it into Polish before you?**

– I've been thinking about translating the Quran for a long time, but I couldn't dare. After all, this is a big deal, a big challenge for the translator. Our Mufti Tomasz Miśkiewicz pushed me to do this. He said, " Try it!" And I dared.

It was really hard but beautiful work, which took three years. I worked day after day, from morning till late at night. As soon as I started, it was impossible to break away. Sometimes I didn't understand phrases well, sometimes I found it difficult to formulate them identically... but I didn't give up. And what is the feeling like when you reach the goal! Joy, emotions cannot be described.

I took the Russian translation of Fazil Karaogly, but I used others, including those of I. Krachkovsky, V. Porokchovaya, E. Kuliev, as well as Czech and English translations. To the best of my ability, I have checked a lot in the original Arabic text. In particularly difficult places I addressed the mufti, who gave me a lot of valuable advice.

The first Polish translation of the Koran was published in 1858. For many years they believed that it was made by a Polish Tatar, but recent studies have shown that its authors were two Catholic Poles. Subsequent translations were released in 1986, 1990 and 2011.

My translation was published by the Muslim Religious Union in the Republic of Poland in 2018. Subsequent editions appeared in 2020 and 2021. I believe that the work of translating the Holy Book was a test that the Almighty gave me.

The latest translation is dated 2021, its author is Rafal Berger, the chief imam of the Association of Muslim Unity (Shiite organization).

It is of interest that in 2017, scientists from the Center of kitabistik studies at Torun University found out that the first translation of the Quran into Polish dates back to 1686. It was made by Polish Tatars and recorded in Arabic in the so-called Minsk Tafsir.

**– Many Tatars, as well as Turks in general, consider themselves Muslims, but do not adhere to Islamic canons, do not speak their mother tongue… Can a modernised Islam that adheres to the basic principles of religion and turns a blind eye to others be right?**

– In my opinion, the most important thing is to accept and adopt all the principles of Islam. We must believe that they are unchangeable and it is our duty to live with them. We must follow all of them according to our capabilities and never lose hope and faith. There are people who pray five times a day, but, unfortunately, this sometimes does not help. I think that faith is not only a prayer, but most of all is our daily behavior, our every action, every thought… We must know our mother tongue. However, the Almighty has sent down different languages to the world so that a person can preserve his culture, customs,.. and at the same time we got the opportunity to study different languages to understand each other.

It seems to me that many modern people have lost control over their behavior. For example, it has become commonplace to post very personal, even intimate photos and events on social networks. Children and teenagers do not listen to their elders and do not respect them. Adults allow young people to do anything. Family values undergo destruction. The Almighty has created nothing supernatural for the people, nothing beyond their abilities. Islam should not be modernized – people should change themselves .

**– How were Tatars perceived in Poland before and what do Poles know and think about them now?**

– Despite the fact that Poland often fought with the Crimean Khanate and Turkey, the Tatars were perceived as brave and courageous people whom they fought but respected as well. Poles and Tatars were allies very often, and the Polish gentry entered into brotherhood with the Tatar murzas and elders many times. During various rebellions in the Golden Horde and then in the Crimean Khanate the Tatars always found refuge in the Polish Crown. They received land in exchange for military service, they also performed important functions – ambassadors, translators, couriers... They had their own units in the Polish army, their mosques and their imams. Polish Tatars were not only soldiers, but also lawyers, doctors, scientists, artists...

Before World War II nineteen Muslim communities and seventeen mosques were located in Poland. Islam was considered the principle and native faith. Poles knew and appreciated their Tatar neighbors. Today it is the same way. There are many words in Polish that come from Tatar (or from Turkish via Tatar), for example, – bow, caftan, divan, sofa, bunchuk... The Poles appreciated Tatar food, weapons, clothes, horses... The Tatars created the most famous Polish cavalry – the uhlans. Their name comes from the surname of the regiment commander Alexander Uhlan (the first half of the XVIII century).

Currently, Poles willingly read books on Tatar history, often in search of their own ancestral roots. The old Tatar villages of Kruszyniany and Bohoniki are often visited, with the only ancient wooden mosques in Poland – historical monuments. Tatars are valued here for their patriotism, devotion to duty and their moral values.

**– Please tell us about your Tatar community in Poland.**

– Currently, about five thousand Tatars live in Poland. In fact, there are many more of them, but many Tatars simply consider themselves Poles and have no real contacts with the Tatar community. The majority, about two thousand, live in the north-eastern part of the country, in the Podlasie. There are two of our historical mosques and Tatar cemeteries there. In 2021, another mosque was opened – in Bialystok, where the active life of the Polish-Tatar community is concentrated.

A large group of Tatars lives in Gdansk, where there is a mosque built in 1990. Gdansk is also a residence of the National Cultural Center of the Polish Tatars. Tatars are scattered almost all over Poland, living in Warsaw, Poznan, Bydgoszcz, Wroclaw, Krakow.

Since I left the army in 1995, I have been working in my community. We have a great team, thanks to which we undertake various public, educational, socio-economic projects and implement them. Many of them are initiated by Mufti Miśkiewicz a nd Barbara Pavlits-Miśkiewicz heads the publishing team and organizes various cultural events. Other examples of the activities of our community members: Rosalia Bogdanovich translates Muslim literature into Polish, Krzysztof Edem Mukharsky makes photos of our diverse life, his wife Anna Hanifa Mukharskaya directs the Tatar children's and youth ensemble ' Bunchuk' . And the historian Alexander Miśkiewicz collects new information about the Tatar life of the past for publication in our magazines. The activity of representatives of the older generation – Dzhemila Smaykevich-Murman, Galina Shakhidevich and Omar Murza Asanovich is remarkable. Thanks to them, our historical traditions and customs are preserved with us.

We have been living on Polish land for more than six hundred years and will live by the will of the Almighty for another thousand years.

**– How are your quarterly magazines ' Tatar Review' and ' Yearbook of Polish Tatars' distributed?**

– Our magazines are distributed to all the centers belonging to the Muslim Religious Union in the Republic of Poland. We send our literature around the country (and abroad too), distribute it to the representatives of the Tatar community, and deliver it to university libraries. We use book fairs and various cultural events for distribution. Not only Polish Tatars are interested in the magazines. Thanks to our publications, many Poles find many useful things for them, restore family ties, and learn some features of the history of their country.

**– Recently, you have begun to actively cooperate with the writers of Tatarstan. From what side does modern Tatar literature attract you and how can it be of interest to European readers?**

– Indeed, I translate stories and poems by Tatar authors. The modern literary work of Tatars is not well known in Poland, although there are many books with Tatar motifs, both in historical terms and in novels. Tatar writers speak beautiful, imaginative language, they have a great literary culture. They know what the main task of literature should be – to have an intellectual and moral impact on readers, to show the true history of the people, to focus their attention on topical issues of our time, to give knowledge and spiritual strength to young generations.

I wish that Polish Tatars become familiar with the works of Gabdulla Tukay, Musa Jalil, Hassan Tufan, Gumer Bashirov, Amirkhan Eniki, Nurikhan Fattah... as well as of contemporary authors. I am not only wishing but also working on it. Last year, for example, a collection of short stories ' Tatar Hearts' was published, where I translated the stories of Lenar Shayeh, Akhat Mushinsky into Polish and placed my own stories next to them. It aroused great interest, and the second, expanded edition under the same name has already been published. A collection of my poems in Tatar is also being prepared for release in Kazan.

**– Your biography says that you and your son translated Tatar folk fairy tales into Polish and published three books. Thus, the continuity of generations is preserved from the point of view of creativity, isn't it?**

– Yes, the translation and publication of Tatar fairy tales was an important event not only for me and my son, but also for our entire Tatar community. Later I participated in many meetings (on Polish radio, in a jazz club), during which I read these fairy tales. In 2012, the Nogai fairy tale theater was founded in Radomsko, inspired by one of the collections of fairy tales that we translated. The young people prepared several performances, which were enthusiastically received at the festival of small theaters.

The popularity of Tatar fairy tales is evidenced by the fact that in 2013 a CD was released with music and six fairy tales that I read. In 2018, the Muslim Religious Union released another album called ' Hushabye from Tatar sky' , where I read ten fairy tales. There are eleven pieces of music among the fairy tales inspired by Tatar folklore.

Fairy tales are an important and very rich element of national culture and traditions, as well as the memory passed down from generation to generation. In my youth, I read fairy tales of different peoples with great interest and pleasure. Then I read fairy tales to my sons, and they read them to their children.

**– Your wishes to the compatriots.**

– My main message is: let's be ourselves. We have a great history and great culture. We can be proud of the achievements of our ancestors. It depends only on us how much of this we will be able to preserve and use for the benefit of the whole people, no matter where anyone lives.

Let us be one big family! Tatar literature should be known in different languages!

# NATALIA KHARLAMPYEVA:
# "THE MATTER OF SURVIVAL
# IS IMPORTANT..."

*As you know, Tatars have very close and deep spiritual, cultural and historical relations with their native Turkic peoples – Turks, Kazakhs, Kirghiz, Bashkirs, Chuvash... But there are also the northernmost, related Yakuts who live thousands of kilometers from Kazan. Recently, our cultures have become much closer.*

*It all started in 2015, when we were invited to Yakutia – to the III International Poetry Festival ' Grace of the Big Snow', which was organized by the People's Poet of the Republic of Sakha (Yakutia), Chairman of the Board of the Union of Writers of Sakha (Yakutia) Natalia Kharlampyeva.*

*In 2016 the Tatar book publishing house issued a collection of poems by Natalia Kharlampyeva ' Kozge yangyrlar' (' Autumn Rains' ) translated into Tatar. In 2017 our dear Yakuts published an Anthology of modern Tatar poetry in the Yakut language. In 2020 the Yakut book publishing house ' Bichik' (now ' Ayyar' ) issued my book for children ' Who lives where?' in Russian, the same year our publishing house issued ' An Anthology of Yakut Poetry' in Tatar. In 2021 and 2022 the Days of the Republic of Sakha (Yakutia) in the Republic of Tatarstan and the Days of the Republic of Tatarstan in the Republic of Sakha (Yakutia) were held in a turn. By the last event, substantial anthologies of modern prose of our peoples were published*

*I talked to Natalia Ivanovna Kharlampyeva.*

– **Natalia-khanum, in 2017 the ' Anthology of Modern Tatar Poetry' was published in the Yakut language. How do you estimate it?**

– We have a great interest in the literature of fraternal Turkic peoples including Tatar literature. It is even possible that we have a special attitude to Tatar literature, since historically it has happened that we live in the same realities not for years, but for centuries. We, the northern Turks, feel part of the greater Turkic world, because there is a concept of ' haan tardar' (' attraction of blood' ), apparently, this is the case. In my opinion, the anthology, though small, is solid – it begins with the poems of the great Tukay and ends with modern young poets. The book was distributed widely to the school libraries of the republic. Tatar poetry develops in line with classical canons, images, metaphors, it is philosophical, it reflects the national character... But I would especially stress two things . It is open to the world, it does not lock in an ethnic framework, besides, it is dynamic and up-to-date. Today, these two things are very important in national literature – not to be isolated within ethnic boundaries and to be able to catch the breath of time.

– **In 2018 you came to Kazan for the Tatar poetry festival dedicated to the 132nd anniversary of the birth of the great Tukai, and visited the poet's homeland. What is your impression?**

– I thank my Tatar colleagues for the invitation to the holiday. I was very glad to attend this really national poetry festival. The name of Tukay has been known to us, Sakha, for a long time, because Tukay is a guiding star for all Turkic peoples. Earlier our aksakals used to translate his fairy tales into the Yakut language, and his poetry often appeared in periodicals. In any case, the name of Tukay is not only known to our readers, but it is respected as well. His fate, formation and life are similar to the biography of our classics. But when I went to Kazan, visited his home places, I got a feeling that I didn't know him well enough. Not only the vicissitudes of his hard life, but also creative activity... I reread some of his works this summer. His life was very short, and he has done so much! People stand in the rain when they read poems at the foot of his monument, they do not go. In a single impulse, they stand up and sing his song, which has become the unofficial anthem of the Tatar people. The oracular word of Tukai lives, unites and inspires.

**– It is well known that only male nightingales sing in the wild, and females do not. What is your attitude to this law of nature regarding poetry?**

– There have been no women poets in our literature for a long time. There were prose writers. Although our people have ancient singing traditions and women's songs occupy a special place in it. It happened that a woman was an object, but not an actor in Yakut poetry. And it was only in the early 70s that Varvara Potapova, a poetess, appeared, who convinced us that the Yakut woman had her own view of the world, her own vision of life. She crossed the threshold and opened her doors to us… When I first gave my poems for discussion, the famous poet, the head of the seminar exclaimed: " Bihigi buhun kyystannybyt!" , that is, "a girl was born today…"

Now, in the decline of my years, I understand that the feminine word, the feminine principle, turned out to be in demand in Yakut literature then. Today, there are probably more poetesses than poets… And sometimes some of them count more on their gender, although literature is a world with male rules. I tell them: " You will be greeted with admiration until you become on a par with real poets, writers, and as soon as this starts, they will demand in a manly, tough manner, without sentiment. Therefore, we should never forget that literature is a man's occupation, just like war and hunting" … I have accepted these rules. But I don't think I write better than men. I do it my own way, not like they do.

**– What is it like to be a national poet of the Republic of Sakha (Yakutia) and at the same time chairman of the Union of writers of the republic?**

– Being the chairman, of course, is not easy. It is impossible to rule writers at all, they are all freedom-loving people. I see the task of the union in creating conditions for creativity, assistance in publishing books, traveling and organizing translations. It doesn't always work out, but I try. In Kazan I was delighted with the support of writers from the state – the building is magnificent, they have transport and literary awards… It's not quite like that with us. Our Head of the republic, Aisen Sergeevich Nikolaev, grew up in the bosom of Yakut literature, his parents are rural teachers, and he supports writers.

I am the first woman in the republic awarded with the title of ' National Poet' . It obliges. Our aksakals have always been on guard of the interests of their people, I follow their course. Time will tell whether it will be a success.

**– How did you get into literature, what was the impetus for you, that amazing spark?..**

– We, Sakha, believe that talent and skill are inherited. Be it a jeweler, a skilled seamstress, a woodworker… The same is with the masters of the Word. My grandfather was *an olonkhosut*, epic performer, improviser. Apparently, my talent is connected with him, although I did not see him, he died before I was born. My mother was an amazing person – she truly was a master of the Word. Comparisons, apt words, sayings, proverbs, fairy tales – I have absorbed all this starting from childhood. She unfolded proverbs for me having educational goals… There is such a Yakut proverb: " Salang kihitten hara tya maha kytta ytyyr" (" Even a tree in the taiga cries from incompetence" ). I asked her, why is it crying? " Someone is not even able to cut it down properly, that's why it's crying" , my mother replied. I was amazed: the tree knows that it will be cut down and does not want an incompetent to cut it... Probably from there, from my family, from childhood, my abilities, my poetic vision of the world comes... In high school all this began to form into poetry – after all, it is easier to write than to be understood verbally when young. I remember the feeling of disaccord between reality and how it should actually be, at its best. And today I am driven by this feeling...

–**Following Nekrasov's question " ho lives well in Russia?" , I would like to ask: " What is it like to live five thousand kilometers away from Moscow, in the Far North?" Ever frost and poetry... How do they combine?**

– Poets, unfortunately or fortunately, always see further... Our land is rich in natural resources – diamonds, coal, gold, oil, gas, tin, even uranium... In the Soviet times this was extracted and went to the center as raw materials. The construction of processing plants was not even thought about at that time. Little has changed now, we are a raw material republic, large corporations like Gazprom, Transneft, Surgutneftegaz, Mechel extract raw materials on the territory of our republic, and we receive taxes. Only in ALROSA we have our own interests as owners. And now we process diamonds on the spot. Although in the early 90s they told us that diamond cutting is simply impossible here, it's not worth thinking about establishing a cutting industry. But our guys, who shot a squirrel in the eye, mastered this business very quickly. Today our gem cutters take prizes at gem cutting contests in Israel.

The future sometimes seems bleak, because you can't draw from nature endlessly, it's not a bottomless barrel. It can respond with environmental disasters, what will be left for our children and grandchildren then? Our nature is very vulnerable, and this is due to eternal frost. But we live on this earth, love it and trumpet it...

– The Yakuts are an ancient people who have preserved their customs, traditions and the Turkic spirit, which is well reflected in the

Yakut literature. I was convinced of this in 2015, when I came to the 3r d International Poetry Festival at your invitation. How do you estimate the current state of the Yakut literature? Who is following your generation?

— Recently, the onset of mass culture has been keenly felt, and this is reflected in literature. There are women's romance novels, detective stories, and our own hunting tales. Fast-selling light reading for one day. This poses a great threat to the future of literature, for those young writers who are just getting on their feet now. It is not difficult to gain popularity on such reading material, and talented guys can follow this easy path. This is a threat to all national literatures.

Yakut literature is developing today according to its own internal laws, we are northerners, unhasty people, that is why our writers are now more focused perhaps on the historical subject, we look back and wish to see the road to tomorrow in the past. There are young people for whom we have great hopes. By the way, the union periodically holds republican meetings of young writers, where new names are discovered. Cinema is developing at a good pace in our republic, so young people are joining the cinema little by little.

— **In my interviews I ask all Tatars this question: " What is your vision of the future of the Tatar language, literature and the nation as a whole?" And what kind of future, in your opinion, awaits the Yakut people? Literature and language? Culture? As we all know: all national languages are going through a very difficult period.**

— This is our common pain! According to the UNESCO data, 25 languages disappear in the world every year...A lot is being done in our republic to preserve not only Yakut, but also other languages of the peoples of the North, which are much smaller in comparison with Sakha. But you know that problems arise when learning languages at school... I believe that today the family is mainly responsible for preserving their mother tongue, only the family can give their mother tongue to the child and give awareness of the need to know it, to preserve it! I don't see any other way in the given circumstances that are not changing in our favor. Everyone should understand that if his child does not speak his mother tongue, then this is the beginning of the end.

**– What is Natalia Kharlampyeva thinking and writing about today?**

– I am thinking about the resilience of my people, about their sharp sense of justice… The people who have mastered the vast northern spaces, became the guide of the empire up to Alaska, created a special northern civilization, they confidently accept the challenges of the modern world, they are ready to bypass the sharp corners and survive. Unfortunately, from century to century, the question of survival of the people has always been the principal one. Today, perhaps, the issue of survival in spiritual, moral and linguistic aspects is more important… I am thinking about it and writing about it.

# ABOUT THE LITERARY WORK
# OF THE AUTHOR

## "ONE OF YOU"
### On the Creative Activity of Lenar Shayeh
### and His Poetic Book Published in London.

> **I'm over twenty now,**
> **And I have started gaining strength.**
> **It's all manhood now,**
> **That makes my soul poetic.**
> *(Translated by Dana Zheteyeva)*

Lenar Shayeh, who once wrote this, happens to be approaching his fortieth milestone...

When one is asked a question: " Who is a poet?" , we usually hear a simple definition: " A poet is an individual who writes verses and is engaged in poetry" . But let us try to look a bit deeper: " Who is a true poet?" If we are speaking of the Tatar poetry, we will first of all recall Gabdullah Tukai. Undoubtedly, he is a genial poet, but it was not him who stood at the origins of the Tatar poetry. The beginning of the Tatar poetry is believed to be connected with the name and the time of Qol-Ghali. But he too is not the originator of the Tatar poetry. The founders of this kind of activity in the history of the Tatars were the ancient folk poets. It means that if we want to find an answer to our question we should study the function, mission, and role of these poets. Called by people the *yerau*, these singing poets have lived among the Turkic Tatars from the time immemorial. They played an important role not only in the Tatar poetry, but also in the public and political life of the people. They decided upon the disputable issues that arose between the tribes, contributed to the consolidation of the friendly and kin relations, and called for peace and cooperation. They were invited to every wedding and to every *jien* (gathering). When necessary, they united people against an enemy, raised them to defend their independence. They had great influence, their ideas and ideals penetrated deep into the soul of the people.

While the *yerau* existed until the second half of the 16th century, later their functions were performed by the *chichyans*. Like the *yerau*, the *chichyans*, being the folk poets and philosophers, teachers and historians, occupied the place of honour as *aksakals* of their country. However, the *yerau* took more care of the interests of the people than the *chichyans*. (Perhaps, it was the first manifestation of the decreasing strength of the Word in the history of the Tatars.) It is known that the tradition of reading the maqams and dastans was on the verge of oblivion with the Tatars. Somewhat later, the meaning of the word ' chichyan' has become narrower to define a master of the art of declamation, a master of ceremonies at dinner parties, an improvising singer of deft tongue and an orator. Obviously, there were reasons for that.

> **Oh, how I wish we could reduce to dust**
> **All of these cars!**
> **Replace the car age,**
> **Bring back to roads**
> **Horses with tarantasses!**

– said Lenar Shayeh. In his other verse, titled the ' Turkic Tunes' we cannot but also notice the following lines: ' The dombra would begin to play…' , ' The kuray would begin to play…' , ' To hear the kubyz…' . It is known that the ancient verses, the dastans, were performed by the yerau and the chichyans to the accompaniment of dombra, dutar, kubyaz, or saz. This music is accompanying the modern poet too:

> **And disputing with ages,**
> **I will wipe off the stints.**
> **And dividing that pie**
> **I'll collect them piece by piece.**
> **With Tatar-proud blood**
> **I was born to this world.**
> **Then, it means we are the same**
> **As Turkic folk.**
> **Bring to me**
> **My raven-black steed!**
> **It's the time of my Turks,**
> **It's the fame of my Turks,**
> **That awaits me ahead!**
> *(Translated by Dana Zheteyeva)*

This means that all thoughts of the poet are about his people, about his motherland. This is the main mission of the *yerau-chichyans*! At least, the poet should be striving for it. At present, the very word ' *chichyan*' is passing out of use, remaining in his works only. Disputable is even the place of the Verse and the Poet in modern society...

Living in the world of stone and iron is, of course, quite difficult for the poetic word. Lenar Shayeh is constantly looking for it (the verse titled ' Post-Modernism' ). Like Tukai, he is concerned about it. The soul of the poet cannot stay indifferent to the world without poetry.

> **I cannot ask for peace inside my exhausted soul.**
> **Indeed, even if the goal is close I cannot reach it.**

**It's not time to blow like the wind, or soar as a bird,**
**But, like a spring I find bliss for my spirit.**
*(Translated by Dana Zheteyeva)*

The poet looks back to the past with nostalgia, but he is the poet of his time and attempts to look into the future. He derives strength for his creative work in the history, culture, and aspirations of his people side by side with the other modern *yerau-chichyans*:

**Looking at the mountains – be that mount yourself.**
**Have great health until you're old.**
**Thank heavens for a sound and healthy nature**
**Omor-aga: then everything's alright.**
*(Translated by Dana Zheteyeva)*

– writes the poet in his verse titled ' Looking at the mounts' , which is dedicated to Omor Sultanov, an *akyn* of the Kirghiz people.

In my opinion, having lived in need and in hardships, Tukai was happy – he freely expressed his thoughts through poetic words . In a ' prison of peoples' , the poet used freethinking to the full measure of his talent.

For example, my mentor, Mudarris Aglyamov, who wrote a foreword for my book of verses several years ago, said the following about it: Patient in life, Sibgat-aga Khakim has once said matter-of-factly the bitter words concerning me and Zulfat: " It turns out that Musa Jalil, Fatikh Karim were happy. They passed away feeling safe that a Tatar child would be growing up as a Tatar child" .

Of course, he will, but only if he does not lose his roots. Not only Sibgat-aga Khakim, who was looking to the future with hope, but also Zulfat and Mudarris-abiy, were happier than us. That was the time of hope ... And man, as is known, lives first of all with hope. When a people gives birth to true poets, who live with thoughts about it, such people are alive and will live.

...Having read the book by Lenar Shayeh titled ' One of You' that was published in London in 2017 by the Eurasian Creative Guild (by *Hertfordshire Press*), I was lost in memories and thoughts about the fate of our people and its poetry. It was the verses of Lenar that prompted me to do this, made me, as they say, stop and look back.

The book, as can be seen from its title, is in English, which means that it is a translation. However, it is well known that no matter how good the translation is, it cannot equal the original. Some translations are weak, some are of high quality. I can say that Lenar is a happy poet, because his verses in this book are translated at a high level. The mastery and efforts of Dana Zheteyeva as a translator have helped to convey in the English language the figurativeness, sonority, and the harmony of the Tatar verses of the poet. No wonder that David William Parr y, the editor of the book and the author of the foreword, the British poet and playwright, member of the Royal Society of Arts, titled his article ' Impressive Tatars' . Indeed, the book by Lenar Shayeh has in full measure announced to the world of the big Turkic-Tatar poetry and sparked interest in it.

Lenar Shayeh is the poet who is able to see and feel the depth and beauty of the word. He possesses the gift of being in unity with different manifestations of nature and man, he feels acutely the seasons of the year and the times of epochs and centuries. In this connection, the title of his collection, ' Moments That Are Lost in Ages' , which was published by the Tatarstan Book Publishing Company in 2016, also proved to be impressive, in my opinion.

The poetic word of Lenar Shayeh represented in 'One of You' is like a stone that was thrown to water, creating the waves that move from one meaning to another, from the individual «'me' towards the natives expanses, towards the feeling of the comprehensive love for his people and the whole world.

> **And he might lead you to the sun,**
> **Your dear timid escort…**
> **While the Sun lives – if you still don't know:**
> **Not in a matchbox, for sure.**
> **Oh, you'll never disappear, my leaf.**
> **I feel it… and I know it…**
> **So, you could be warmed up,**
> **While I warm the world with my love.**
> *(Translated by Dana Zheteyeva)*

> **Such is the true goal of the true poet…**
> **If you are ready to give for a good cause**
> **The joy and the zeal of your labour**
> **Then the name of yours**
> **Will be shining forever.**

So be it! I wish Lenar Shayeh, who treats the strength and the grandeur, the sorrows and the griefs of his people, his motherland, and of mankind as his own, and who has expressed them in his art with the great poetic force, the new creative achievements and the heights of the *yerau-chichyans*!

*Rustem Sulti,*
*Tatar poet, London, 2019*

www.ingramcontent.com/pod-product-compliance
Lightning Source LLC
Chambersburg PA
CBHW040759180626

R18458200001B/R184582PG46815CBX00001B/1